Alasdair G

Scottish Cultural Review
of Language and Literature

Volume 4

Series Editors
John Corbett
University of Glasgow

Sarah Dunnigan
University of Edinburgh

James McGonigal
University of Glasgow

Production Editor
Gavin Miller
University of Edinburgh

SCROLL

The Scottish Cultural Review of Language and Literature publishes new work in Scottish Studies, with a focus on analysis and reinterpretation of the literature and languages of Scotland, and the cultural contexts that have shaped them.

Further information on our editorial and production procedures can be found at www.rodopi.nl

Alasdair Gray
The Fiction of Communion

Gavin Miller

Amsterdam - New York, NY 2005

Cover design: Gavin Miller

The paper on which this book is printed meets the requirements of "ISO 9706: 1994, Information and documentation - Paper for documents - Requirements for permanence".

ISBN: 90-420-1757-0
©Editions Rodopi B.V., Amsterdam - New York, NY 2005
Printed in The Netherlands

Contents

Acknowledgements	7
Introduction	9
Chapter One: *Lanark*, *The White Goddess*, and "spiritual communion"	21
Chapter Two: The divided self – Alasdair Gray and R.D. Laing	53
Chapter Three: Reading and time	87
Conclusion: How "post-" is Gray?	115
Bibliography	135
Index	141

Acknowledgements

For their assistance in the reviewing and production of this book, I would like to thank John Corbett, James McGonigal and Cairns Craig. I would also like to thank Bob Irvine, Richard Canaday and Tanith Muller for their comments and suggestions. Any errors that remain are my responsibility.

Some of the arguments in this book have appeared in an earlier form in *Studies in Scottish Literature*, *Psyart*, *Journal of Narrative Theory* and *Edinburgh Review*. My thanks go in particular to the reviewers of these periodicals, whose comments have proved extremely valuable.

Finally, I would like to thank Alasdair Gray for generously answering various of my questions, and also for providing an image for the cover of this book.

Introduction

In the early 1980s, Scottish literature underwent a period of regeneration in which Glasgow was a focus for new writers. Alasdair Gray was foremost amongst these voices. Although he had published little, Gray was an accomplished visual artist and playwright, and had been Writer in Residence at Glasgow University. *Lanark: A Life in Four Books* (1981), his first published novel, made an extraordinary impact upon Scottish literature, releasing a torrent of new writing from authors such as James Kelman, Janice Galloway, Tom Leonard and Liz Lochhead. Since *Lanark*, Gray has produced further novels and collections of short stories, as well as occasional political pamphlets and poetry collections. Alongside his work as a writer, Gray has continued to work in the visual arts. This expertise is apparent in his books: they are marvels of typography complemented by his own illustrations.

Life

Alasdair James Gray was born in Glasgow on 28 December 1934 to Alexander and Amy (née Fleming). Gray's father worked in a box-making factory; his mother was a shop assistant for a clothing firm. The family were working class, but lived in a modern and well-designed housing scheme quite unlike the extreme deprivation of neighbourhoods such as the Gorbals. After the outbreak of World War Two, bombing raids on Glasgow forced the family to evacuate to various locations outside the city. They finally settled in Yorkshire, where Alexander Gray worked as a hostel manager. The Gray family returned to Glasgow after the war, and it was there that Alasdair completed his education.

While at school, Gray's precocious literary and artistic talents were evident. As a high school student, he had stories published in *Collins Magazine for Boys and Girls*, and read his verse on BBC Radio. However, in a biographical piece from the collection *Ten Tales Tall & True* (1993), Gray recalls his dislike for the utilitarian emphasis of the Scottish educational system:

Compound interest, sines, cosines, Latin declensions, tables of elements tasted to my mind like sawdust in my mouth: those who dished it out expected me to swallow while an almost bodily instinct urged me to vomit. (Gray 1993: 156)

The psychosomatic connection is no exaggeration: Gray suffered asthma attacks and eczema from early childhood until after graduation from art college. His psychological stress was further intensified by the death of his mother in 1952, while he was still a teenager.

Gray successfully completed high school despite his problems. Although his family did not have enough money to support his education, Glasgow School of Art arranged financial support in order that he could attend. He specialised in design and mural painting, but wrote throughout college, and worked on sections of what later became *Lanark*. He graduated in 1957, and began a journey through Spain funded by a travelling scholarship. An account of this journey would later be published in "A Report to the Trustees of the Bellahouston Travelling Scholarship" collected in *Lean Tales* (1985).

Gray returned to Scotland, and supported himself as a part-time high-school teacher while working on various mural projects for the remainder of the 1950s. In 1961, during a stint as a scene-painter in the Edinburgh Festival, he met his first wife, Inge Sørensen. They soon married, and had a son, Andrew, in 1963. Gray briefly brushed with fame in 1964, when he was the subject of a BBC TV documentary, *Under the Helmet*. Payment from this programme allowed Gray to support himself in various artistic ventures. He also received a regular source of income throughout the 1960s and 1970s by writing radio and TV plays.

In 1972, Gray joined a creative-writing group run by Philip Hobsbaum, a lecturer in English Literature at Glasgow University. There, Gray met other Glaswegian writers such as Tom Leonard, James Kelman, and Agnes Owens. Five years later, his steadily increasing literary profile led to an appointment as Writer in Residence at Glasgow University from 1977–1979. This was something of a shock to his colleagues in the art world, where he was regarded as a visual artist who worked in portraiture, book design and murals. Elspeth King, the former curator of the People's Palace museum in Glasgow, recalls Gray's announcement in 1977 that he was leaving his post as artist recorder: "This came as a shock and disappointment. It seemed to be a waste of his time and talent as an artist" (King 2002: 112). However, during his period at Glasgow University, *Lanark: A Life in Four Books* was accepted for publication by Canongate. Its eventual appearance in 1981 was Gray's impressive debut on the literary scene. Most authors build up to their magnum opus. Gray's delayed entry into the literary marketplace meant, however, that his first published work was his largest and most significant. Its impact upon the Scottish literary scene is hard to overestimate. The novelist and reviewer Allan Massie declared in *The Scotsman* that *Lanark* was "a quite extraordinary achievement, the most remarkable thing done in Scottish fiction for a very long time. It has changed the landscape" (Massie 1981).

In the 1980s, due to the success of *Lanark*, Gray no longer needed to earn a living from activities outside of art and literature. He published two collections of short stories: the highly regarded *Unlikely Stories, Mostly* (1983), and, with James Kelman and Agnes Owens, the less substantial *Lean Tales* (1985). As well as writing another acclaimed novel, *1982 Janine* (1984), Gray continued to write scripts, publish poetry, and develop earlier work into prose fictions such as the novelistic collage, *Something Leather* (1990). The latter, though, was not as successful as its predecessors. Gerald Mangan in *TLS* concluded that it was a book whose "argument is as superficial and incoherent as its characters". This was largely due, Mangan observed, to Gray's propensity to recycle work: "very few chapters make any effort to conceal their unrelated origins as stories and plays" (Mangan 1990).

Gray, who had separated from his first wife in the late 1960s, married again in 1991 to Morag McAlpine. In the following years he published two novels, *Poor Things* (1992) and *A History Maker* (1994), as well as a collection of short stories, *Ten Tales Tall & True* (1993). *Poor Things* joined *Lanark*, *1982 Janine*, and *Unlikely Stories, Mostly* as Gray's finest literary works. Elizabeth Young in *The Guardian* announced that "this new book is his most substantial since *Lanark*", and applauded it as "a bibliophile's paradise of postmodern precision" (Young 1992). At around the same time, Gray also entered the political arena with *Why Scots Should Rule Scotland*, a pamphlet advocating Scottish independence.

After the publication of the short-story collection *Mavis Belfrage* in 1996, Gray produced little original literature. The rather slim size of the volume led John Sutherland to observe in his review for *TLS* that "*Mavis Belfrage* continues the curious diminuendo in Alasdair Gray's career since the monumental achievement of *Lanark*" (Sutherland 1996). Gray was busy instead with artistic activities or with his longstanding project to compile an annotated anthology of literary prefaces.

Gray's publishing history shows an unusually long time-lag between composition and publication. Parts of *Lanark*, for example, were written in the 1950s. He has also frequently reworked plays into prose fiction: *The Fall of Kelvin Walker* (1985), *McGrotty and Ludmilla* (1990), and *Something Leather* all re-employ scripts from Gray's early career. In the epilogue to *Something Leather*, Gray is disarmingly frank about the homogeneity of his work:

> A few years ago I noticed my stories described men who found life a task they never doubted until an unexpected collision opened their eyes and changed their habits. This collision was usually with a woman, involved swallowing alcohol or worse, and happened in the valley of the shadow of death. I had made novels and stories believing each an adventurous new world. I now saw the same pattern in them all – the longest novel used it thrice. (Gray 1985b: 232)

Alasdair Gray's career as an author seems to be drawing to an end. The frequency and size of his publications have gradually declined in the two decades since the initial impact of *Lanark*. Gray's *The Book of Prefaces* (2000) anticipated his appointment in 2001 to a Chair of Creative Writing at the University of Glasgow, a post which he shared with James Kelman and Tom Leonard, two writers whom he had known since his membership of Hobsbaum's creative-writing group in the 1970s. In 2003, Gray resigned his post as Professor of Creative Writing in order to return to painting. His most recent publication is the collection *The Ends of Our Tethers: 13 Sorry Stories* (2003).

Re-grounding Gray in Scotland

In this book, I argue that Gray's work deserves to be situated within Scottish culture, for there are many important (albeit undervalued) Scottish thinkers and writers who helpfully illuminate his writing. It seems to me that without such a re-grounding of Gray in Scotland, his work is likely to be understood as a rather tardy imitation of international "postmodern" literature.

My approach might appear to imprison Gray's writing within nationalist literary criticism. There seems a danger that my analysis could prevent more forward-looking readings. As Eleanor Bell has pointed out: "Scottish literary studies have been more focussed on canon-building and the construction of the national tradition, and too immersed in tradition-inspired approaches to take account of [...] theoretical developments" (Bell 2004a: 86). Situating Gray in his context might therefore seem to be a step backwards, for there is still at large in Scotland an old-fashioned genealogical style of criticism which traces domestic poets and authors back through their Scottish lineage. The aim is to construct an ethnic family tree through which the pure blood of the Scottish tradition flows: outsiders and bastards (in practice, "the English") need not apply; despite any accidental residence in, or association with, Scotland, foreigners and "hybrids" are not true Scots. Furthermore, if this bloodline is, for example, masculine, heterosexual, and oriented towards the folk or the working classes, then certain interpretations and certain texts are closed off. As Christopher Whyte has argued, the homoerotic potentials of canonical texts such as Walter Scott's *Redgauntlet* (1824) and Muriel Spark's *The Prime of Miss Jean Brodie* (1961) are excluded (see Whyte 2004); and, as Anne Scriven has pointed out, the entire *ouevre* of the nineteenth-century novelist Margaret Oliphant disappears from view (see Scriven 2004).

An assumption of cultural "essentialism" is therefore allied to the construction of Scottish literary "ethnicity". As Diana Fuss puts it: "an essentialist assumes that innate or given essences sort objects naturally into species and kinds" (Fuss 1990: 5). Add a twist to the essentialist position – that artificial productions also sort essentially into kinds – and we have the assumption behind certain monolithic literary critical practices. References to a Scottish tradition or context (whether in culture generally, or merely in literature or ideas) seem to invite a metaphysical position in which Scottish cultural artefacts share a common essence which is necessary to their existence as works that are specifically Scottish. In an essentialist view of Scottish literature, the individual differences between texts so designated – genre, length, apparent subject matter, and so forth – are accidental variations on a single man-made species defined by characteristics such as the antithetical psychology of the "Caledonian antisyzygy" offered by G. Gregory Smith (see Smith, G. Gregory 1919), or by less explicit criteria based, for example, on masculinity, heterosexuality, the presence of folk or popular culture, and so forth.

The essentialist position therefore disadvantages Scottish literature because it offers a homogeneous category. For the essentialist, every "truly Scottish" literary text is composed of the same uniform stuff. To an anti-essentialist, however, "Scottish Literature" is simply a convenient term which gathers together a variety of different texts, none of which need have any relation to a supposed "essence" of Scottishness. Such "nominalism" responds to the risks of an essentialist approach to Scottish literature that may obscure the individual features of "Scottish" texts, occlude international literary relations, and ignore whole areas of "marginal" Scottish writing.

Yet, although anti-essentialists make important arguments, their anxieties are, I believe, overstated. Critics may indeed prescribe essentialist accounts of Scottish literature; this does not mean that they are ever wholeheartedly employed. Essentialism and anti-essentialism are two theorisations of an ongoing practice; they are not themselves that practice. The natural sciences continued despite various deficient accounts of what scientists did (such as, for example, British Empiricism during the Enlightenment, or logical positivism in the twentieth century). Similarly, Scottish literary criticism has probably been less influenced by its own self-conscious reflections than might be supposed: accurate description of what went on, rather than theoretical debate, could settle this issue.

A further point can be made in response to anti-essentialist criticism. Although Scotland could never be regarded as a wholly colonised culture, the unequal Union with England has certainly led to a degree of "inferiorisation" – an assumption, amongst Scots, that the culture of their country is less worthwhile than that of their larger, dominant partner. To a certain extent, this attitude was shrugged off in the Scottish Renaissance of the 1920s and 1930s. Some inferiorist attitudes persisted however. The Renaissance often inverted, rather than overcame, the binary distinction between English and Scot. As I have argued elsewhere, the Scottish Renaissance tended to take on board mythologies about the Scottish character (and language), and proclaim the superiority of this inferiorised Scottishness over the supposed essence of the English:

> In the poetic tradition started by [Hugh] MacDiarmid, continued by [Robert] Crawford, and analysed by [Derrick] McClure, the discourse of the Scot is presented as inherently vivid, forceful, emotive, vigorous and embodied – as an antidote, in short, to the supposed intellectual detachment of the English. Yet what seems to be an act of resistance to English cultural domination is little more than acquiescence in the imaginary binaries of inferiorism. The colonisers have already declared themselves to be rational, thoughtful, and cultured, in opposition to the colonised who are irrational, passionate, and primitive. (Miller 2004a: 206)

Insofar as Scottish canon-building has promoted essentialism, it is often because of a lingering Scottish inferiorism. The supposed impassioned, vigorous, manly, populist "essence" of Scottish literature is itself an inferiorist symptom no more helpful to Scots than the parallel assertion that African Americans have "natural rhythm".

We need not rush from an allegedly essentialist critical position to an enthusiastic investigation of every context for Scottish literature that is "beyond Scotland". We need, in fact, to continue the Renaissance response to English cultural domination by further situating Scottish literature in Scotland. In particular, the essentialism of Scottish literary criticism will (although this may seem paradoxical) wither and weaken as we investigate how individual Scottish writers relate to Scottish thinkers – the recovery of Scottish ideas will discredit the myth of the anti-intellectual essence of Scottish literature.

That Scottish ideas are so rarely investigated in Scottish literary criticism is a particularly absurd inferiorist symptom – as shocking, for example, as considering the work of Albert Camus or Jean-Paul Sartre without reference to French existentialism. Cairns Craig has noted that

to imply that it is only through the ideas of Russian or American intellectuals [e.g. Mikhail Bakhtin and Charles Taylor] that one can grasp the real nature of the Scottish condition is to continue Scotland's submission to cultural imperialism rather than fulfil its "post-colonial" identity, reproducing the inferiorism by which Scotland is always the object of an understanding that can only come from outside Scotland itself, never a subject capable of understanding itself. If we, in Scotland, are not simply to be the consumers of the cultural paradigms promulgated in the globalised economy of the modern intellectual arena, we have to take account of what the traditions of Scottish thought provide, both towards the interpretation of Scottish culture and as contributions to our current international environment. Becoming properly "post-colonial" in a Scottish context would involve a re-grounding of our intellectual life in the traditions of Scottish culture. (Craig 2004: 241)

The international cultural paradigm most often associated with the work of Alasdair Gray is that of "postmodernism". The assumption that Gray is a paid-up postmodernist is made by Brian McHale in his seminal *Postmodernist Fiction* (1987). He regards Gray's use of various narrative and textual devices as an attempt to disclose the essential fictionality of the so-called "real" world. *Lanark* then fits neatly into McHale's supposition that postmodern writing is primarily concerned to enlighten us about the fictionality of our own consensual reality, and therefore to provide an anarchic "refusal either to accept or to reject any of a plurality of available ontological orders" (McHale 1987: 37). It is not just McHale's paradigm of plural worlds to which Gray's work is assimilated. Donald P. Kaczvinsky provides an equally straightforward reading of *Poor Things* in terms of a philosophical assault on historical "objectivity": "Like Alasdair Gray's more famous novel *Lanark* […], *Poor Things* […] presents a postmodern metanarrative" (Kaczvinsky 2001: 775). To Kaczvinsky, *Poor Things* is an exercise in "historiographic metafiction", the aim of which is to expose the fancifulness of historical truth. "What is fact and what is fiction in *Poor Things* is up for grabs" (Kaczvinsky 2001: 791); behind the claim for "objectivity and truth" is a mere "fictional construct" (Kaczvinsky 2001: 790).

To such arguments I will return in my conclusion, where I consider some of the "post-" categorisations which have been applied to Gray's work. The reading offered in this book, however, will involve many ideas which are not part of any "post-modern", "post-structuralist", or even "post-national" intellectual context. I pay particular attention to an intuition which, it seems to me, is part of an ongoing (but neither exclusive, essential, nor total) tradition in Scottish literature and ideas: namely, the idea that human life is essentially social, that human beings need each other for recognition and acknowledgement – for, in other words, "communion". My use of this word may seem rather odd and anachronistic. To many readers, it will summon up images of Christian worship: communion, in its most familiar sense, is Holy Communion, in which the Eucharist (the consecrated bread and wine) is distributed amongst worshippers. A whole host – no pun intended – of arcane disputes surrounds this ritual, but few modern readers are likely to have much interest in whether the bread and wine in fact turns into the body and blood of the Son of God ("transubstantiation") or whether they, in some equally mysterious way, co-exist ("consubstantiation"). The term "communion" and the familiar associations which surround it seem to offer little that is promising for literary interpretation and criticism.

But strip "communion" of its (to some, anachronistic or superstitious) holiness, and the secular meaning of the word comes into focus: that of "sharing", "participation" and "fellowship" in a common experience or life. We are members of a community because of the things we do that bring us into a common life with each other. Within the vocabulary of "communion" there is a whole range of suggestive metaphors and etymologies. One of the things that we share in order to participate in a common life is food. We have companions because we break bread with them: the etymology of "companion" is the Latin prefix *com-* plus the Latin for bread, *panis* (*Concise Oxford Dictionary* 1976: 205). With our companions, we are members of a common life, a "corporation" or metaphorical body (Latin *corpus*), of which each individual is joined as a limb or "member". And if we recognise our companions, it is not just because they are familiar faces, it is because to recognise, or acknowledge someone, is to create a common life with them, to see them as equal, dignified – as kindred.

It is on this sense of communion – that of recognition, of establishing a common life – that I will focus in this book. We can meet with others in various ways according to the different media of communion. The paradigm, of course, is a ritualised meal – eating together is a well-established cultural form which establishes a group as a company. We can also think of other rituals which create and form groups (of all sizes): love-making, dancing, games, collaboration, worship, and so on. Through such rituals we recognise others as fellows who are members of our communities. This is distinct from treating them as "aliens" or "outsiders", to whom we do not extend our common life (typical examples of those who are aliens in this way have included slaves, women, criminals, foreigners, the sick and the mad).

The concept of "communion" may so far seem fairly easy to understand. Communion, however, is a phenomenon that has often been obscured by theories about society. This is a point to which I will return, but I will here briefly indicate some of the issues. There is a long tradition of analysing society through the fiction of a self-sufficient individual. This is, for example, the thought-experiment proposed by Thomas Hobbes in his early-modern political treatise, *Leviathan* (1651): what would make society aggregate together if each man were allowed to be entirely free and self-governed? His answer is that men would still band together because of the advantages of security and protection that would accrue to each member of a society. This methodological fiction can often settle down into an assumption that human beings really are essentially asocial, and that they exist in communities only for the secondary benefits that such associations bring. Even analyses which seem to have a lot to say about society often therefore have little to say about any inherent sociability in human beings. For all Marx's criticism of alienation and exploitation within capitalism, he did little to analyse social relations other than economic relations of exchange. Freud, too, had little sense of community as a primary reality. His model of psychological development is one in which, under the threat of a mythical "castration", an essentially egoistical and hedonistic infant matures – or is repressed – into an adult whose sexual desires are directed towards others.

Some of the few detailed studies of communion were those provided by Victorian social anthropologists such as William Robertson Smith (1846–1894) and J.G. Frazer (1854–1941). Robertson Smith's understanding of communion is central to his anthropology, and provides a convenient illustration of the range of the concept. In his article on "Sacrifice" in the ninth edition of *Encyclopaedia Britannica*, Robertson Smith treats sacrifice as prototypically a communion meal: "God and worshippers make up together a society of commensals [i.e. table-sharers]"; indeed, "the stated and normal intercourse between gods and men has no other form" (Robertson Smith 1878–1889: 134). Sacrifice, to Robertson Smith, is a basic social ritual (eating together) specially extended so that the God may also participate. By this means the God becomes a member of the basic community – the "kindred"– and enters into "the circle of social duty and reciprocal moral obligations" (Robertson Smith 1878–1889: 134). Indeed, so powerful is this concept that Robertson Smith sees sacred communion as the essential form even of national religions, which he regards as "developments or combinations of the worship of particular kins" (Robertson Smith 1878–1889: 134).

In another work, *Kinship and Marriage in Early Arabia* (1885), Roberston Smith again finds communion – this time without any transcendent participation by a deity – in his description of "kinship", the primal social relationship: "all kinship", he writes,

> was originally through women; generally speaking the mother and nurse are one, and the bond of birth is confirmed by the continued dependence of the suckling on the nourishment that it draws from the mother's body. (Robertson Smith 1907: 176)

As this analysis emphasises, kinship is not a biological fact, but a social relation constituted by a ritual of communion. So, for example, another ritual (the "morning draught") is required to bond father and son:

> the mere act of procreation does not make a bond between the father and the child to whom he has never given the morning draught [...]. The father's morning draught given to his boy acquires the same significance in constituting kinship as mother's milk had formerly done, after the weight formerly given to the bond of motherhood is transferred to fatherhood. (Robertson Smith 1907: 177–78)

To such ideas, I will return in future chapters. In particular, the opposition between a communion which is secular and bodily, and a spiritual communion (to which a God or other transcendent power is invited), will prove particularly fruitful.

Robertson Smith (like Frazer, to whom I will also make reference), was Scottish. It is interesting to note several recent observations that communion is something of particular significance for students of Scottish culture. Michael Gardiner in *The Cultural Roots of British Devolution* (2004) has emphasised the importance of the Scottish philosopher John Macmurray (1891-1976), whose work he sees as amongst Scotland's responses to its colonial position. One of Macmurray's key political and philosophical ideas, notes Gardiner, is that of communion between persons, "pragmatic, individualistic society is overcome in the first instance by a [...] mutuality between persons – recognition" (Gardiner 2004: 85). Macmurray's role in establishing the importance of recognition has also been noted by Cairns Craig in his survey, *The Modern Scottish Novel* (1999). Craig picks up Macmurray's idea that "the Self is neither a monadic thinker nor a pragmatic economic unit [but] is constituted in, through and by its relationships to others" (Craig 1999: 90) – this concept Craig designates "heterocentricity". The idea allows Craig to develop detailed readings of canonical Scottish texts such as Nan Shepherd's *The Quarry Wood* (1928). As the protagonist, Martha, is removed from her small rural community to study at Aberdeen University, she is equally isolated from her fellows. What ensues is not a traditional novel of struggle towards authenticity, but rather a movement in Martha's life towards a "recognition of the self's communitarian basis": "her real self is not to be constituted by negating the peasant community of her relatives [...] but in the fulfilment of the community in and through which her self is constituted" (Craig 1999: 92). Craig also sees a similar pattern – though one of failure of community – in Lewis Grassic Gibbon's trilogy *A Scots Quair* (1932-1934), where Chris Guthrie's narrative progress is marked by a reduction of her society to a mere pragmatic aggregation, rather than a congregation like that which so frequently assembles in the first volume, *Sunset Song*. By the final volume, *Grey Granite*, we have seen a "decay of self-hood from the full acknowledgement of the other that is a person into the selfish egoism of an economic individualism" (Craig 1999: 96).

I, too, have been interested in re-invigorating the substantial body of Scottish ideas surrounding communion and community. In my monograph, *R.D. Laing* (2004), I discuss in detail the philosophical and psychoanalytic background to the work of Scotland's most famous psychiatrist (see Miller 2004b). I will return to these ideas later in this book, but some anticipation of Laing's concepts and context is useful. Laing, like Macmurray, regards human life as essentially social. His first book, *The Divided Self* (1960), is a study of what happens to the self when it is unable to find meaningful communion with others. The self-division Laing discusses is not that over-familiar Jekyll and Hyde complex (the Caledonian anti-syzygy) which has so often been attributed to the Scots. Instead, it is a division between disembodied "mind" and a mechanised "body". The body forms an "outer" self, to which are delegated transactions with a meaningless and frustrating community. The mind, on the other hand, roams in a fantastic realm of spontaneity, and posits in this inner life imaginary social relationships more hospitable to its individual being. This "schizoid" response to unfulfilling community will provide a particularly fruitful motif for analysis. My reading of Gray will focus on a particular form of imaginary personal relationship – one in which the projected communion is conducted with or through a higher power or reality, and so becomes something closer to Holy Communion (or to the sacrificial communion described by William Robertson Smith). Whether in religion, philosophy, or literary criticism, we can often find doctrines – with varying degrees of explicitness – that posit a higher world that is neither spatial nor temporal. This higher world can provide a culturally-sanctioned location for the kind of schizoid imaginary relationships that I will detect in many of the readings which follow.

Chapter One

Lanark, *The White Goddess*, and "spiritual communion"

Gray's first published novel, *Lanark: A Life in Four Books*, has often been regarded as a work of postmodern literature. The final book in particular contains many of the standard characteristics of the genre. Lanark meets his own author, and has also to travel through a mysterious, seemingly postmodern "Zone" of the kind examined by Brian McHale. Such a reading tends, though, to neglect the first two books of *Lanark*, with their focus on realistic narrative and character psychology. It would be easy to simply regard these books as a modernist warm-up to the postmodern main event in Books Three and Four. I believe, though, that a closer examination of the realist books of *Lanark* reveals some very traditional humanist concerns which underlie an extensive critique of modernist literature. The overall pattern of the first two books is one of an escape from human relations via the projection of an imaginary other who validates the protagonist's spontaneous life. This attempted "schizoid" solution founders because of the ethical and psychological consequences which afflict Duncan Thaw.

Original sin

If – as I argue – Gray's fiction shows characters who develop a "schizoid" relationship with the world, what is wrong with the communities from which they withdraw? Why do Gray's characters so often end up conducting imaginary personal relationships? The answer is found in Gray's depiction of Scottish culture: he shows a stifling ethos – one which is latently religious – at work in Scottish communities. Where there should be freedom and spontaneity, there is instead a guilty submission, as if the fact of one's existence were in itself an embarrassment. One way to escape such self-castigation, Gray shows, it to seek out a higher community – one which annuls guilt, and permits exemption from cultural imprisonment.

A stifling patriarchal Scottish community is readily apparent in texts such as *1982 Janine*. Jock McLeish, the protagonist, drunkenly recalls his past as he lies on his bed in a hotel room somewhere in Scotland in the early 1980s. Interspersed with his sadomasochistic fantasies, and defying his attempts to repress his memories, come fragments of his upbringing. Jock wonders if "Mad Hislop", his old schoolteacher, may have been his biological father – there is some suggestive evidence in Jock's pre-marital conception and his noted resemblance to Hislop. Jock's suspicion is not confirmed anywhere else in the narrative, and so its accuracy remains undecidable for interpreters. On the other hand, Jock's suspicion is at least figuratively perceptive: Jock is initiated into Scottish manhood by his relationship with Hislop. Ritualised punishment with the tawse – a leather strap – is the rite of passage by which a boy comes to be acknowledged as a man. Jock recalls how, after Hislop returns to teaching after the death of his wife, he abruptly singles Jock out for punishment because of the latter's "condescending" gaze of sympathy (Gray 1985a: 85). Despite the pain of the tawse, Jock stifles his cries, and even asks Hislop to continue: in response "[Hislop] smiled and nodded, slipping the Lochgelly over his shoulder under the jacket. He said gently, 'Go to your seat son. There's a spark of manhood in you'" (Gray 1985a: 85).

As Jock, rather unwillingly, reflects on this scene, he alludes to a theological significance in such ritual humiliation: "'The Lord Chastiseth whom he loveth', says the bloody old Bible" (Gray 1985a: 86). The reference is to Paul's epistle to the Hebrews: "For whom the Lord loveth he chasteneth, and scourgeth every son he receiveth" (*The Bible* 1997: Heb. 12.6). For Jock to be recognised as a legitimate Scottish male, he must be chastised by Hislop, just as God scourges those who would enter his kindred:

If ye endure chastening, God dealeth with you as with sons; for what son is he whom the father chasteneth not?
But if ye be without chastisement, whereof all are partakers, then are ye bastards, and not sons. (Heb 12.7–8)

The sacred tawse has, we might say, replaced Robertson Smith's more innocent and profane "morning draught".

The theological parallel extends further. The boys who are beaten so arbitrarily by Hislop acquire a mysterious guilt: "I did not tell my mother that he had belted me because I believed that getting hurt that way was a shameful thing" (Gray 1985a: 82). This inner conviction of worthlessness persists into manhood: the adult Jock remarks, "There is evil in me, which is why I deserve whatever I get" (Gray 1985a: 60). Such "original sin" is a way of making sense of arbitrary cruelty: only by assuming some mysterious culpability, can Jock retain his trust in the justice of his godlike teacher.

Jock's consequent self-loathing blights his adult life. While a student, Jock begins a relationship with a young woman called Denny whom he meets in the refectory of the college that he attends. He abandons her, however, for the seemingly more glamorous Helen, whom he comes to know while working as a technician in a theatrical production at the Edinburgh Festival. Jock's guilt at his neglect and betrayal of Denny is compounded when Helen informs him (mistakenly, or perhaps deceptively) that she is pregnant. Jock is soon paid a visit by Helen's father, who, like Hislop before him, represents the Judaeo-Christian religion: "as Mr Hume stonily raved and thundered like Moses on Mount Sinai he was talking about Denny, although he did not know it" (Gray 1985a: 299). His diatribe preys upon Jock's feeling of original sin:

I must have already suspected I was shit for Mr Hume's words completely crushed me. I saw that I was a dirty bit of stupid wickedness and it was right that three men were flexing their muscles to punch me. (Gray 1985a: 299)

Although Jock does not love Helen, he sees her supposed pregnancy as the proverbial "accident" sent to punish him for betraying Denny. He accepts his lot, and expresses an inauthentic desire to marry Helen: "I said softly, 'Please inform your daughter that I love her dearly and will marry her whenever she feels it best that I do so'" (Gray 1985a: 300); what Jock might want, as opposed to the expectations of his society, ceases to be a concern – "I felt that what I was no longer greatly interested me" (Gray 1985a: 300).

The problem for Duncan Thaw, the protagonist of *Lanark*, is how to avoid Jock's fate – for the latter is gradually assimilated to the technocratic ethos of his society, until his dull conformism leads to the crisis depicted in *1982 Janine*. Duncan, from the start, is much more openly rebellious. His resistance to the demands of his society – mediated through his parents – creates a childhood conflict which revolves around rituals of communion: "[Mrs Thaw's] son always refused shepherd's pie or any other food whose appearance disgusted him: spongy white tripe, soft penis-like sausages, stuffed sheep's hearts with their valves and little arteries" (Gray 1987: 123). The punishment for this refusal is much like that administered, in the name of Fatherly love, to Jock McLeish:

[Mr. Thaw:] "Tell her [your mother] you're sorry and you'll eat what you're given."
Then Thaw would snarl "No, I won't!" and be thrashed. (Gray 1987: 123)

Not even a sound Scots thrashing, however, is quite enough to deter Thaw. Accordingly, his parents take to immersing their son in a bath of cold water, which effectively subdues him. This parodic baptism forces Thaw to participate in the sacramental rituals of his latently religious society.

The christological and anthrotheophagous ("man-god eating") overtones of the "shepherd's" pie are also suggestive:

> He stared at the mushy potato with particles of carrot, cabbage and mince in it and wondered if brains really looked like that. Fearfully he put some in his mouth and churned it with his tongue. It tasted good so he ate what was on the plate and asked for more. (Gray 1987: 124)

The sacramental pie – baked in a gas oven used in the suicide of a previous tenant – is a symbolic rite of passage by which Thaw enters into the ethos of his culture.

Yet Thaw can maintain a critical distance from his culture and its expectations because of another childhood communion – one which eventually replaces the sacraments of his latent national religion, but which also, in the end, damages his personality and perverts his art. One day, Thaw follows a group of children whom he meets as they rake through domestic refuse. They tease and harass him, and he runs away crying, lost in unfamiliar territory:

> The dark, similar streets seemed endlessly to open out of each other until he despaired of getting home and sat on the kerb with his face in his hands and girned [groaned] aloud. He fell into a dwam [daze] in which he felt only the hard kerb under his backside. (Gray 1987: 128)

It seems that his cry of despair is answered. A heavenly force – matriarchal, and therefore distinct from the Judaeo-Christian deity – manifests itself in order to guide him back to his homeland:

> [he] awoke suddenly with a hushing sound in his ears. For a second this seemed like his mother singing to him then he recognized the noise of waterfalls. The sky had cleared and a startling moon had risen. Though not full there was enough of it to light the canal embankment across the road, and the gate, and the cinder path. (Gray 1987: 128)

The moon, perceived animistically by Thaw's childish mind, then appears to vent its wrath as he follows the path home during an air raid:

> Thaw seemed to hear the moon yell at him. It was the siren. Its ululations came eerily across the rooftops to menace him, the only life. He ran down the path between the nettles and through the gate and past the dark allotments. The siren swooned into silence and a little later (Thaw had never heard this before) there was a dull iron noise, gron-gron-gron-gron, and dark shapes passed above him. Later there were abrupt thuddings as if giant fists were battering a metal ceiling over the city. (Gray 1987: 128)

Yet, as if by some providence, Thaw is soon re-united with his family, and spared from the anger of the moon: "Beyond the power station he ran his head into the stomach of a warden running the other way. 'Duncan!' shouted the man" (Gray 1987: 129).

This experience is so remarkable because Thaw disobeys his father's commands, but avoids the usual rituals of a thrashing and a cold bath:

> Thaw was very uneasy. His adventure with the midden-rakers was a horrider crime than not eating dinner so he expected punishment on an unusually large scale. After closely watching his mother that day [...] he became sure that punishment was not in her mind, and this worried him. He feared pain, but deserved to be hurt, and was not going to be hurt. He had not returned to exactly the same house. (Gray 1987: 129)

Although his parents are merely relieved that he is alive, it seems to Thaw that he has found a relationship which annuls his own inner sinfulness. After his encounter with the moon, Thaw therefore fantasises of himself as a prophet in order to continue his sense of divine exemption. To some extent, he employs motifs borrowed from Judaeo-Christian culture. For example, he transforms his evacuation from Glasgow into an escape from a flood: "It struck him that the sea was behind these hills; if he stood among the trees he would look down on a grey sea sparkling with waves" (Gray 1987: 130). His mother assures him that this is untrue, but he cannot shake off the forceful image: "The sparkling grey sea was too vivid for him to disbelieve. It fought in his head with a picture of farms and fields until it seemed to be flooding them" (Gray 1987: 131). Subsequently, at the rural hostel to which he is evacuated, Thaw models himself after Moses, leading the chosen people to the Promised Land – or even Christ leading the redeemed to Heaven:

Thaw trudged along the coast road at the head of a mob of about thirty or forty [...]. He wanted to seem mysterious to these boys, someone ageless with strange powers, but his feet were sore, he was late for tea and afraid he would be blamed for arriving with so many friends. He was right. The hostel gateman refused to allow the other boys in. (Gray 1987: 132)

These Judaeo-Christian motifs are, however, transplanted into a worship of the feminine deity who saved Thaw during the air-raid. Thaw is disappointed by the local girls who "were all too obviously the same vulgar clay as himself" (Gray 1987: 135), so he settles upon an Artemis-like figure in an advertisement: "when visiting the village store he saw a placard in the window advertising Amazon Adhesive Shoe Soles. It showed a blond girl in brief Greek armour with spear and shield and a helmet on her head" (Gray 1987: 135). The pursuit of this figure drives Thaw to climb nearby Ben Rua, despite his father's injunction not to do so unless suitably equipped:

On the grey-green tip of the summit he seemed just able to see a figure, a vertical white speck that moved and gestured [...]. To Thaw the movement suggested a woman in a white dress waving and beckoning. He could even imagine her face: it was the face of the girl in the adhesive shoe-sole advertisement. This remote beckoning woman struck him with the force of a belief, though it was not quite a belief. (Gray 1987: 140)

The incarnate moon summons Thaw, approving of his desire to climb Ben Rua like some sandalled Biblical prophet. When Mr Thaw learns of this adventure he is pleased, despite himself, at his son's sudden burst of physical activity:

His father looked at his sandalled feet and said, "If you do it again you must tell someone you're going first, so we know where to look if there's an accident. But I don't think we'll complain this time; no, we won't complain, we won't complain." (Gray 1987: 145)

Again, though, Thaw has been spared a thrashing or a cold bath because of a manifestation of the moon goddess. Mr Thaw's leniency merely confirms unwittingly his own subordination to her will.

As Thaw grows older, he intensifies his fantasy life in order to preserve a sense of exemption from the demands of his culture. At primary school, back in Glasgow after the war, "[Thaw] told long stories with himself as hero [...]. The vivid part of his life became imaginary" (Gray 1987: 134). The vocabulary here alludes to a quotation which Thaw stumbles across from David Hume's *A Treatise of Human Nature*:

All the perceptions of the human mind resolve themselves into two distinct kinds, which I shall call IMPRESSIONS and IDEAS. [...] These perceptions, which enter with the most force or violence, we may name impressions; and under the name I may comprehend all our sensations, passions and emotions, as they make their first appearance in the soul. By *ideas* I mean the faint image of these in thinking and reasoning. (Gray 1987: 161)

In the *Treatise* itself, Hume admits that his phenomenological distinction is not absolute:

In sleep, in a fever, in madness, or in any very violent emotions of soul, our ideas may approach to our impressions: [...] on the other hand it sometimes happens, that our impressions are so faint and low, that we cannot distinguish them from our ideas. (Hume, David 1978: 1)

The distinction between perceiving and imagining blurs: impressions may become as dull as thoughts, and ideas may have the vivacity of feeling. By such an inversion of vivacity, Thaw refuses to ascribe reality to his embodied existence:

Apparent life was a succession of dull habits in which he did what was asked automatically, only resenting demands to show interest. His energy had withdrawn into imaginary worlds and he had none to waste on reality. (Gray 1987: 157)

Much of Thaw's life is led in daydreams of secular soteriology, such as his fantasy that he is an immortal mutant survivor of a third world war:

In two or three centuries of wandering about the shattered earth he had become leader of a small group of people [...]. He had brought them to the crater, protected by its walls from the envy of a bygone age, to build a republic where nobody was sick, poor or forced to live by work they hated. (Gray 1987: 158)

Thaw's ongoing sense of divine inspiration allows him to maintain a core of authenticity behind his superficial assent to the pragmatic life of his society. This preserved sense of spontaneity fosters his adolescent rebellion against his allotted role. By dint of talent, stubbornness (and some providential good fortune), he successfully enters art college, and escapes the fate which awaits his schoolfriend Coulter. The latter reflects on his job in a shipyard: "At first the novelty made it not too bad. It was different from school, and you were getting paid, and you felt a *man*" (Gray 1987: 215). A real man must – like Jock McLeish – surrender all inclinations which are without technical utility: "engineering isnae compulsory", says Coulter, "I chose it. And I'm a man now. I have tae take it seriously, I *have* tae keep shoving my face against this grindstone" (Gray 1987: 216).

The White Goddess

The story of Duncan Thaw undoubtedly has some biographical inspiration. Thaw's psychic withdrawal into a seemingly more fulfilling inner life has its own parallel in Gray's upbringing. Although this psychological genesis for Gray's fiction may be of interest to biographers, a more interesting interpretation relates Thaw's psychology to the literary culture of the twentieth century. An incident in Thaw's personal religion hints at some of the connections. Instead of getting to know ordinary teenage girls, he is infatuated with his blonde classmate Kate Caldwell because she resembles his goddess. In a scene where Thaw complains to Coulter about the hopelessness of his love, we find him obsessed with his inner, imagined lover: "Thaw walked onward with a small perfect image of Kate Caldwell smiling and beckoning inside him" (Gray 1987: 175). Thaw's subsequent pursuit of this image leads to a quite extraordinary scene of dendrophilia:

> It was possible to imagine that the trunk between his arms contained the body of a woman. He hugged it, pressed his face against it and whispered, "I'm here. I'm here. Will you come out?" He imagined the woman's body pressing the other side of the bark, her lips wrestling to meet his lips, but he felt nothing but roughness. (Gray 1987: 176)

Such behaviour is, as the anthropologist J.G. Frazer might remind us in *The Golden Bough* (1922), appropriate to a worshipper of Diana:

> the mortal King of the Wood had for his queen the woodland Diana herself. If the sacred tree which he guarded with his life was supposed, as seems probable, to be her special embodiment, her priest may not only have worshipped it as his goddess but embraced it as his wife. [...] Even in the time of Pliny a noble Roman used thus to treat a beautiful beech-tree in another sacred grove of Diana on the Alban hills. He embraced it, he kissed it, he lay under its shadow, he poured wine on its trunk. Apparently he took the tree for the goddess. (Frazer 1987: 8)

I have briefly mentioned Frazer in connection with William Robertson Smith, but he is, of course, already well known as amongst the inspirations for T.S. Eliot's *Wasteland* (1922); references to *The Golden Bough* appear in Eliot's notes to the poem. Indeed, Frazer's social anthropology had a far wider and greater impact upon culture and literature than Robertson Smith's. John B. Vickery declares,

> *The Golden Bough* [...] has become one of the most influential works in the twentieth century. What is most striking is the depth to which it has permeated the cultural strata of our time. In literature alone it touches everything, from the most significant to the most ephemeral works. (Vickery 1973: 3)

Among those influenced are "William Butler Yeats, T.S. Eliot, D.H. Lawrence, Edith Sitwell, Naomi Mitchison, Robert Graves, Richard Aldington, Archibald MacLeish, John Peale Bishop, Ezra Pound, and Caroline Gordon" (Vickery 1973: 74). Literary modernists were particularly impressed by Frazer's massive investigation: Vickery, for example, analyses D.H. Lawrence's writings, and concludes that "the majority of his works through image, scene, action, or allusion embrace nearly every major notion concerning myth and ritual to be found in *The Golden Bough*" (Vickery 1973: 309). Scottish writers too – of a broadly modernist persuasion – also found inspiration in Frazer. Cairns Craig has shown how authors such as Robert Louis Stevenson, Neil Gunn, and Muriel Spark developed Frazer's analysis of the "rituals and legends of a world more ancient and more enduring than anything in the annals of civilisation" (Craig 1999: 149).

Such "primitivist" use of Frazerian ideas often led, though, to unhappy poetic and political corollaries. T.S. Eliot's 1919 essay "War Paint and Feathers" contains a fine statement of the importance of primitivism to modernist poetry: the poet "is the most and the least civilized and civilizable; he is the most competent to understand both the civilized and the primitive" (cited in Craig 1982: 131). The poet, for Eliot, has to comprehend the continuity between primitive and civilized in order to be master of the associations that his writings will create with the (equally continuous) culture of his desired audience. As Cairns Craig has put it, "to find some way of controlling the associative flow in the reader the poet had to know with what kind of memory his poem would engage" (Craig 1982: 71). Yeats, too, has a similar attitude. His poetry requires a public in touch with what Richard Kearney calls "an idealized Celtic paganism *pre-existing* the colonial rupture of Ireland" (Kearney 1997: 113) – "a mythic religion founded on the Collective Unconscious of the race" (Kearney 1997: 114). Writing for such an audience, Yeats can, for example, safely gloss the execution of the leaders of the 1916 Easter Rising as a "mythic rite of blood sacrifice" (Kearney 1997: 114).

A problem arises, however, when the audience proves unreceptive to the profound meanings expressed by the poet. Not everyone accepted the idea, for example, that the soil of Mother Ireland was being watered by the blood of her martyred sons. Eliot, too, would find himself disturbed by those whose free-thinking made them unwilling to accept the tradition that awaited his individual talent. His hostility to Jews is symptomatic; as Anthony Julius argues, it often exploited "a type largely of anti-Semitism's own invention, the anarchic, intellectually subversive Jew" (Julius 1995: 146). Consequently, Yeats and Eliot (and also Pound) were, in Craig's words,

> driven to politics in order to maintain the institutions and the patterns of society which preserved and promulgated the kinds of memory on which their poetry relied. The open poem demanded for its completion not the free mind of democratic man, but the rich mind of the privileged within a hierarchical society. (Craig 1982: 71)

Yeats would be fascinated by the Blueshirts; Eliot flirted with fascism; and Pound, notoriously, allied himself to Mussolini.

Of the connection between primitivism, twentieth-century art and right-wing politics, Gray himself is quite aware. In the short story "The Great Bear Cult" (1983), a struggling photographer in the 1920s begins a movement in which members dress as brown and black bears. This superficially comical tale alludes to the rise of pre-war British fascism in the form of the "brownshirts" and the "blackshirts". When the human bears attack Labour Party buildings, "The police remain aloof until the riots are nearly over and most of the people they arrest are left-wing and furless" (Gray 1984b: 60). What has largely gone unnoticed is that *Lanark* also engages with primitivist art and authoritarian politics. A precise intertextual relationship with *Lanark* is provided by the Frazer-influenced work of the poet Robert Graves (1895–1985), who provides a striking parallel to Thaw's mentality in his book, *The White Goddess,* first published in 1948, and republished in an enlarged edition in 1952. Martin Seymour Smith remarks that Graves's "debts to Frazer (of *The Golden Bough*) [...] have been noted by most commentators" (Smith, Martin Seymour 1982: 387). This may explain why the book was originally accepted by an editor who was himself an admirer of Frazer: "Eventually, it was T.S. Eliot, at Faber, who came to his rescue" (Smith, Martin Seymour 1982: 398).

The White Goddess is a highly speculative anthropological study in which Graves claims to discover the traces of a matriarchal religion which preceded the later masculine and Apollonian religions of the Greeks, Romans and Christians. As Douglas Day makes clear, Graves gave free reign to his imagination in constructing this work: it is

> a curious blend of fact and fancy, an often impenetrable wilderness of cryptology, obscure learning, and apparently *non sequitur* reasoning brought to bear on a thesis that has its roots partly in historic fact, partly in generally accepted anthropological hypotheses, and partly in poetic intuition. (Day 1963: 157)

The work begins with Graves's claim to have revealed in Celtic literature traces of the usurpation of goddess worship by patriarchal religion; he then elaborates what he sees as various parallels with Greek myth, analogies which – he claims – reveal a similar, albeit earlier, process at work. Poets, he then asserts, are the remaining inheritors of the worship of the mother goddess.

The parallels between *Lanark* and *The White Goddess* are striking. (Indeed, Gray has acknowledged his contact with Graves's ideas: "I read *The White Goddess* with pleasure but did not feel I *needed* women to crucify me into art – tho' with hindsight I recall that some did" (Gray pers. comm.)). Just as Thaw's visual art is predicated upon his affinity with the lunar goddess, so, for Graves, poetic inspiration is precisely the union of the poet's soul with a feminised lunar deity: "Constant illiterate use of the phrase 'to woo the Muse' has obscured its poetic sense: the poet's inner communion with the White Goddess, regarded as the source of truth" (Graves 1952: 446). Graves sees such poetic communion as essential to a fraternal relation with the natural world. A restored kinship with the White Goddess would, he believes, resist the modern assumption that scientific and economic ends are ultimate:

> [Poetry] was once a warning to man that he must keep in harmony with the family of living creatures among which he was born, by obedience to the wishes of the lady of the house; it is now a reminder that he has disregarded the warning, turned the house upside down by capricious experiments in philosophy, science and industry, and brought ruin on himself and his family. (Graves 1952: 14)

The aspiring author who hopes to write poetry by going to creative-writing classes, or through buying a rhyming dictionary, is therefore in for a shock:

> Poetry began in the matriarchal age, and derives its magic from the moon, not from the sun. No poet can hope to understand the nature of poetry unless he has had a vision of the Naked King crucified to the lopped oak, and watched the dancers, red-eyed from the acrid smoke of the sacrificial fires, stamping out the measure

of the dance, their bodies bent uncouthly forward, with a monotonous chant of: "Kill! kill! kill!" and "Blood! blood! blood!" (Graves 1952: 446)

Although Graves's doctrines may seem bizarre, they do agree significantly with the presentation of modern society found in Gray's fiction, where an ascetic Protestantism dominates and suppresses the population through the myth of "original sin". The turning point in Western civilisation can, for Graves, be traced to the victories of this patriarchal sect:

The Civil Wars in England were won by the fighting qualities of the Virgin-hating Puritan Independents, who envisaged an ideal theocratic society in which all priestly and episcopal pomp should be abolished, and every man should be entitled to read and interpret the Scriptures as he pleased, with direct access to God the Father. (Graves 1952: 446)

Graves insists that the eventual consequence of this desacralising and democratising victory is "that money [...] is the sole practical means of expressing value or of determining social precedence; [and] that science is the only accurate means of describing phenomena" (Graves 1952: 468). Much of what motivates Thaw to worship the moon can therefore be found explicitly in Graves's work. There is little place for the artist in a society dedicated to an economic and technical efficiency derived from an austere, patriarchal Protestant religion.

In this critical vision of modern rationality, Graves parallels (but crucially, only to an extent) the more careful critique developed by the German theorists Theodor Adorno and Max Horkheimer. In their study *Dialectic of Enlightenment* (1944), Adorno and Horkheimer discuss how, in their judgement, the Enlightenment of the eighteenth century has developed into a mode of oppression. They point out that Enlightenment thinkers understand a crucial modern advance to be the removal from nature of anthropomorphic projections. The demythicising of the world leads to knowledge of both an inanimate natural order and of the human "I" which experiences it. No longer do "inward impulses appear as living powers of divine or demonic origin" (Adorno and Horkheimer 1979: 89) – they are clearly ascribed to the self which confronts an alien natural world increasingly devoid of intention and significance. Yet, just as the ego is born, so it is destroyed. Since the Enlightenment rejects both passion and tradition as contaminants of reason – "Any other than systematically directed thinking is unoriented or authoritarian" (Adorno and Horkheimer 1979: 82) – then any particular human goal or value is identical with another. All are instances of psychological conditioning by utility or tradition: reason "exposes substantial goals as the power of nature over mind, as the erosion of its self-legislation" (Adorno and Horkheimer 1979: 87). "Good" and "evil", for example, become just two species of psychological compulsion; between them, there is no essential difference. When even fundamental human values are reduced to external compulsion, then "the power of nature" represents "mere indiscriminate resistance to the abstract power of the subject" (Adorno and Horkheimer 1979: 90).

The parallels with Graves are many. He, too, is distrustful of the way in which nature has been evacuated of meaning and significance. Like Adorno and Horkheimer, he traces this process back to the earliest forms of rationalisation: "Socrates", declares Graves, "in turning his back on poetic myths, was really turning his back on the Moon-goddess who inspired them and who demanded that man should pay woman spiritual and sexual homage" (Graves 1952: 11). Because Socrates "preferred to [...] discipline his mind to think scientifically", the processes of rationalisation were set in motion. The end point is an ethic of technical efficiency which today exploits a natural world previously protected by the aura of the sacred:

"Nowadays" is a civilization in which the prime emblems of poetry are dishonoured. In which serpent, lion and eagle belong to the circus-tent; ox, salmon and boar to the cannery; racehorse and greyhound to the betting ring; and the sacred grove to the saw-mill. (Graves 1952: 14)

Graves's solution, however, would have appalled Adorno and Horkheimer – for it is in the same mould as the right-wing politics of Yeats, Eliot and Pound. Democracy, concludes Graves, is itself a symptom of the erosion of substantive values:

Puritanism took root and flourished in America, and the doctrine of religious equalitarianism, which carried with it the right to independent thinking, turned into social equalitarianism, or democracy, a theory which has since dominated Western civilisation. (Graves 1952: 468)

Democracy, for Graves, is an illegitimate employment of the instrumental thinking favoured by the lower-classes:

We are now at the stage where the common people of Christendom, spurred on by their demagogues, have grown so proud that they are no longer content to be the hands and feet and trunk of the body politic, but demand to be the intellect as well – or, as much intellect as is needed to satisfy their simple appetites. (Graves 1952: 468)

In an echo of Hobbes's theory of society, Graves assumes that democracy is a pact between self-interested individuals who so idolise private law that they seek to extend it into public law (in the form of a "social contract"). This is why the speaker of the poem "The White Goddess" embarks on his quest in "scorn" of those who are "Ruled by the God Apollo's Golden Mean" (Graves 1952: 5). For Graves, the reciprocity of the social contract – expressed in the principle "Do unto others as you would have them do unto you" – eventually detaches legality from substantive morality. The law ceases to be the expression of a stable ethic:

> If [...] it is wished to avoid disharmony, dullness and oppression in all social (and all literary) contexts, each problem must be regarded as unique, to be settled by right choice based on instinctive good principle, not by reference to a code or summary of precedents; and, granted that the only way out of our political troubles is a return to religion, this must somehow be freed of its theological accretions. Positive right choosing based on moral principle must supersede negative respect for the Law which, though backed by force, has grown so hopelessly inflated and complex that not even a trained lawyer can hope to be conversant with more than a single branch of it. (Graves 1952: 471)

The common people must therefore be shielded from the temptations of constitutional law, democratic freedom, and human rights. Instead of blindly following the law, the hands and feet and trunk of the body-politic should, Graves argues, blindly follow an ethically gifted elite:

> so few have the capacity to make a proper moral choice between circumstances or actions which at first sight are equally valid, that the main religious problem of the Western world, is briefly, how to exchange demagogracy, disguised as democracy, for a non-hereditary aristocracy whose leaders will be inspired to choose rightly on every occasion, instead of blindly following authoritarian procedure. (Graves 1952: 471)

Graves contends that such "proper moral choice" is provided by worship of the moon-goddess. Only by renewing an animistic attitude to nature can one resist the creeping corruption of free-thinking rationality:

> the word *lex*, "law", began with the sense of a "chosen word", or magical pronouncement [...] But as soon as religion in its primitive sense is interpreted as social obligation and defined by tabulated laws – as soon as Apollo the Organizer, God of science, usurps the power of his Mother the Goddess of inspired truth, wisdom and poetry, and tries to bind her devotees by laws – inspired magic goes, and what remains is theology, ecclesiastical ritual, and negatively ethical behaviour. (Graves 1952: 471)

For Graves, the majority of the population – the "hands and feet and trunk of the body-politic" – can be allowed autonomy only in the sphere of material production and means-end rationality. Their ultimate substantive ends they must accept uncritically from a ruling elite possessed of a sacred authority. Who should comprise this aristocracy? Poets, we will recall, are the priests of the moon-cult. They are the "non-hereditary aristocracy" whom Graves hopes will eventually be the acknowledged legislators of the world.

In Graves's prescription, the clock must go backwards; only by deceiving ourselves that the natural world contains intentions and agency – that the Moon tells us, or our bosses, what to do – can we overcome the apparent tendency of rationality to cut us off from any concrete ethical life. What Graves prescribes in the 1950s, from his villa in Franco's Spain, is, in essence, a fascist political structure. Jürgen Habermas, an inheritor of Frankfurt school thinkers such as Adorno and Horkheimer, discusses the intimate links between pagan religion and fascist spectacles. He refers to features of the "show aspect of fascist leadership"; he lists

> the cultic honouring of leaders as sacred personages, the artfully staged mass rituals, the manifestly violent and hypnotic elements, the breach of legality, [and] the denunciation of even the appearance of democracy and all egalitarian values. (Habermas 1987: 216)

Graves's poet, of whom Duncan Thaw is an echo, is a miniature fascist leader. Were a Gravesian poet ever to obtain effective power, we would find these same elements concretely realised according to the prescriptions in *The White Goddess*. The poet is a sacred aristocrat, the leader of a cult, who understands that "positive right choosing" must supersede democracy and legality, and who appreciates the ritual value of public killing in front of hypnotised followers (with their "monotonous chant of 'Kill! Kill! Kill!'").

It is, quite frankly, astounding that Graves could promote such lunacy (I use the term advisedly) so soon after World War Two. Perhaps, though, we should not judge him too harshly. Primitivism and authoritarianism were not limited merely to Yeats, Eliot, Pound and Graves. Even W.H. Auden seems oddly blind to the fascist associations of renewed paganism. In his "Moon Landing" (Mendelson 1976: 632–33), the speaker sees the Apollo missions as the terminus of scientific mastery over nature: "from the moment // the first flint was flaked this landing was merely / a matter of time" . The speaker proudly declares his resistance to the disenchantment of nature – "my Moon still queens the Heavens / as She ebbs and fulls, a Presence to glop at" – and suggests, contra Enlightenment, that "Irreverence / is a greater oaf than Superstition". Yet somehow it escapes the speaker's notice that "the von Brauns, and their ilk" had worked within Nazi Germany, a society which had already attempted a cultic response to modernity.

The failure of cultic art

Although the narrative of *Lanark* picks up primitivist Frazerian motifs, it also provides a sceptical counterpoint to Graves's authoritarian modernism. *Lanark* is not so much a work of "post-modernism" as a work opposed to modernism. Whatever the spiritual dilemmas of a society enslaved to economic rationality and to the production of unjustly distributed material wealth, a modernist return to mythicism is out of the question. Thaw's worship of his own white goddess, I shall argue, takes over and corrupts his entire existence, so that his life provides a miniature parable for the failure of Gravesian ideas. Both Thaw's art and his social life are destroyed by their subjugation to his personal cult, and this is particularly evident in his treatment of women.

The cancerous spread of the belief system which initially protected Thaw's personality becomes apparent during his time as an art student. When his locker is robbed during his first day at the art college, Thaw's sense of original sin – like that held by Jock McLeish – re-asserts itself as he confesses the loss to his father:

[Mr Thaw:] "What were you afraid of? Did you think I'd thrash you?"
"I deserve to be thrashed." (Gray 1987: 235)

Under the rationalisation of saving to the value of the stolen goods, Thaw puts himself through a self-mortifying penance designed to re-unite him with the moon goddess. He walks to college, eats less and less, and gradually retreats into his inner life – "His mind was clenched, his surface reinforced against surrounding life" (Gray 1987: 228). Shielded from the external world of people and things – "All sounds, even words spoken nearby, seemed dulled by intervening glass" (Gray 1987: 228) – he is in a Humean borderline state in which "our impressions are so faint and low, that we cannot distinguish them from our ideas". This condition allows Thaw to direct more of his energy towards his religious life. The colour yellow, an association with the "gold flake" of the moon (Gray 1987: 160), animates external nature, triggering Thaw's sexual and emotional responses, even as he depersonalises the people around him:

> Yet while he looked on people with the cold interest usually felt for things, the world of things began to cause surprising emotions. A haulage vehicle carrying a huge piece of bright yellow machinery swelled his heart with tenderness and stiffened his penis with lust. A section of tenement, the surface a dirty yellow plaster with oval holes through which brickwork showed, gave the eerie conviction he was beholding a kind of flesh. (Gray 1987: 228)

Thaw then seeks out the incarnation of the lunar goddess in a fellow student, Molly Tierney, a "velvet-voiced girl with blond curls" (Gray 1987: 229). She matches well Graves's ideal: the goddess "whose broad high brow was white as any leper's / Whose eyes were blue, with rowan-berry lips / With hair curled honey-coloured to white hips" (Graves 1952: 5). As Thaw sits with Molly in Brown's cakeshop (as a "commensal" in Robertson Smith's terminology), she seems filled with a divine light:

> Sounds of people moving and conversing at other tables blurred and receded, but tiny noises nearby [...] were magnified and distinct. Molly Tierney came into sharp focus. The colours of her hair, skin, mouth and dress grew clearer like a stained-glass figure with light increasing behind it. Second by second her body was infused with the significance of mermaids on rocks and Cleopatra in her barge. (Gray 1987: 230)

Molly, however, reveals herself to be an illusory incarnation as she begs her boyfriend to complete a project for her: "Jimmy, it's my architecture homework. This model cathedral we've to make. I've tried to make it but I can't, [...]. Will you make it for me?" (Gray 1987: 231). Thaw reacts with vividly imagined contempt for this false idol: "A voice in Thaw's head raved at Macbeth, 'Spit in her face! Go on, spit in her face!'" (Gray 1987: 231). On the walk home, lunar imagery betokens his disenchantment with Molly: "Clock dials glowed like fake moons on invisible towers" (Gray 1987: 231).

If the goddess cannot be found in person, then Thaw must pervert his artistic creativity into the production of religious iconography. He sketches an idea for a painting with "a moon in the sky above the treetop" (Gray 1987: 236). Though the moon eventually disappears from this painting, he still expects his work to "eclipse" that of the others in his year (Gray 1987: 238). He is disappointed, though, to find that there are better, less devotional, works. Nevertheless, a subsequent black-and-white sketch is reproduced in a newspaper. This restores his faith in his contact with the goddess: "the published photograph gave him a moment's pleasure of almost sexual potency. He went over to the refectory in a mood of unusual confidence" (Gray 1987: 246). A fortuitous meeting soon comes Thaw's way as he pursues his favourite colour:

> One evening Thaw came down to Sauchiehall Street when the air was mild and the lamps not yet lit. So fine a lake of yellow sky lay behind the western rooftops that he walked toward them in a direction opposite home and was overtaken by Aitken Drummond at Charing Cross. (Gray 1987: 253)

Because of his attraction to the lunar colour yellow, Thaw meets Aitken and goes with him to the art-school ball, where he meets Marjory Laidlaw. During their consequent low-key, on-off romance, Thaw's adolescent awkwardness is compounded by a religious impulse. Marjory produces what Graves would describe as the "exaltation and horror" excited by the "religious invocation of the Muse" (Graves 1952: 14):

> He sat on the upper deck watching the pure line of her face and throat against the black window. They filled him with delight and terror for he would need to cross over to them and he hadn't much time. He stared desperately, trying to learn what to do by intensity of vision. (Gray 1987: 265)

Thaw's visionary intensity is a consequence of the religious need which lurks behind his relationship with Marjory. Her sexual favours would be an erotic communion with the goddess – he therefore transplants her into Kelvingrove Park, an appropriate sacred context:

> Nearby an almost full moon was freckled by the top leaves of an elm. The river gurgled faintly against its clay bank, the distant fountain tinkled. Marjory said, "Lovely."
> He said, "I've once or twice felt moments when calmness, unity and ... and glory seemed the core of things. Have you ever felt that?" (Gray 1987: 285)

Thaw's attraction to Marjory is as shallow as his pubescent infatuation with Kate Caldwell. He has little interest in Marjory as an individual, and this brings him into line with Graves's injunction that the artist must look beyond phenomenal women in order to unite himself with the ideal reality of the goddess: "Truth has been represented by poets as a naked woman: a woman divested of all garments or ornaments that will commit her to any particular position in time and space" (Graves 1952: 446). Marjory becomes merely a ceremonial object to be exploited in the sacred rituals which have taken over Thaw's artistic powers:

> He stopped and gripped her arm. "Marjory, can I draw you? Naked, I mean?" She stared. He said eagerly, "I won't be embarrassed – my picture needs you." (Gray 1987: 286)

A dream clarifies the solitary self-assertion of his sexuality, which is now almost fully subordinated to his need for a spiritual bond with his goddess:

> Thaw dreamed he was fornicating awkwardly with Marjory, who stood naked and erect like a caryatid. He rode astride her hips, holding himself off the ground by gripping her sides with knees and arms. The cold rigid body stayed inert at first then gradually began to vibrate. He had a thin, lonely sensation of triumph. (Gray 1987: 276)

Marjory echoes an ancient image of feminine subordination. A "caryatid" is "a female figure used as a column to support an entablature": certain classical buildings have used columns carved into female form, with the weight of the stonework bearing down upon the head of the figure. This small narrative detail therefore deconstructs the matriarchal pretensions of Graves's (and Thaw's) primitivism. Etymologically, the word "caryatid" derives from a Greek term for "a priestess of Artemis at Caryae" (*Oxford English Dictionary* 1989: 932) – these moonworshippers were enslaved alongside the rest of the women of the city by the conquering Greeks.

Thaw's treatment of his sister provides a further satiric counterpoint to the Gravesian doctrine that one's "inferiors" – such as women – are merely accidental to the pursuit of the goddess. When Thaw's sister, Ruth, dares to damage one of his paintings, his attacks her, and subsequently offers a perfunctory apology:

> He said coldly, "I'm sorry."
> He could only think of the grey smear on the picture. Coldness and indifference spread through him like a stain. (Gray 1987: 238)

Yet, so long as his painting goes well, Thaw is convinced of the inspirational acknowledgement of the goddess, and that is all that matters. When his work begins to improve, so does Thaw's mood – despite his precarious position within his family:

> Mr. Thaw made tea that evening and the family ate in silence. Inside himself Thaw was very cheerful indeed but hid the feeling because the others could not

share it. Afterward he began the picture again and finished it three days later. (Gray 1987: 238)

Thaw's "commensal" relationship with his family is empty; his real communion is with the imaginary other who inspires his artistic life.

Graves would be proud of Thaw's sense of superiority to domestic existence, and of his relative indifference to the individuality of his sexual objects:

> The White Goddess is anti-domestic; she is the perpetual "other woman", and her part is difficult indeed for a woman of sensibility to play for more than a few years, because the temptation to commit suicide in simple domesticity lurks in every maenad's and muse's heart. (Graves 1952: 447)

Family life, for Graves, opposes artistic creativity:

> The reason why so remarkably few young poets continue nowadays to publish poetry after their early twenties [...] is that something dies in the poet. [...] He has lost his sense of the White Goddess: the woman whom he took to be a Muse, or who was a Muse, turns into a domestic woman and would have him turn similarly into a domesticated man. Loyalty prevents him from parting company with her, especially if she is the mother of his children and is proud to be reckoned a good housewife. (Graves 1952: 447)

When read against *Lanark*, such pronouncements provide an indictment of Graves's response to modern society. Cultic modern art does not resist exploitation; it consolidates the position of those who are the exploiters. The enraptured masses merely furnish a means to the aesthetic life – they make the paint, print the books, and, in the case of a lucky few women, provide the nude models and the poetic muses. The complicity of Graves's assault on modernity with the exploitation which he claims to abhor is most apparent in the attitude of Graves (and Thaw) to women. We find an ironic counterpoint to their doctrines: both are priests of matriarchies where women are silent props for their artistic masters.

Lanark therefore responds to the authoritarian potential which may be perceived in certain primitivist works of modernism. On the one hand, Gray's narrative agrees with the general modernist distrust of the economic and religious foundations of modernity. On the other hand, though, *Lanark* can be read intertextually with Graves's *The White Goddess* as a satire upon the modernist ambition which understands art as the scripture and iconography of an ascendant theocracy. *Lanark* is therefore a didactic text. It informs us that cultic art is little better than the masturbatory power-fantasies which fill Thaw's adolescent imagination.

From the moon to the son

Lanark does not merely undermine cultic aesthetic projects; it also presents, in passing, a response to the problems which drive both Graves and Thaw to their repellent doctrines. *Lanark* gestures, by an implied contrast, towards an ethic which recognises the social and personal world as a value higher than art. The crucial motif is the replacement of sacred communion with everyday rituals of kinship – in Lanark's case, of kinship with his son, Sandy.

Thaw is eventually so depressed by his isolation from real, living others that he kills himself. The Third Book of *Lanark* begins as the amnesiac protagonist is reborn as "Lanark", finding himself adrift in a eerie city, where inhabitants regularly disappear, and where mysterious diseases such as "dragonhide" and "twittering rigour" are endemic. Lanark succumbs to the first of these diseases: his skin begins gradually to scale over into a rigid armour (a metaphor, of course, for the indifference to others which he manifested as Duncan Thaw). Lanark cures himself of this disease by entering the fantastic underground "Institute", an organisation which both attempts to cure the diseased and to exploit the industrial potential of those who cannot be saved. Here he meets, and cures, Rima, a young woman afflicted with dragonhide. Gray's narrative presents Lanark with a chance – through Rima – to escape Gravesian modernism by returning to a mundane life in which both his art and his sexuality may have significance for others.

Firstly, though, Lanark must escape from the ideology of those like Sludden, who controls the biggest clique in the city's "Elite Café", and who subscribes to an axiology of power: "Moments of vivid excitement are what makes life worth living, moments when a man feels exalted and masterful" (Gray 1987: 5). Art, for Sludden, is merely one more means to enter a Gravesian "non-hereditary aristocracy" by having power over people: "An artist doesn't tell people things, he expresses himself. If the self is unusual his work shocks or excites people. Anyway, it forces his personality on them" (Gray 1987: 6). In symbolic response to this ethic is Lanark's search for the sun. Lanark's quest, as Professor Ozenfant of the Institute notes, is opposed to worship of the moon. In typically primitivist fashion, Ozenfant therefore invites Lanark to understand it as a search for a deity:

> you are no Athenian, no Florentine, you are a modern man. [...] As for lovemaking and friendship, humanity has always preferred to enjoy these at night. If you wanted the moon, I could sympathise, but Apollo is quite discredited. (Gray 1987: 78)

Ozenfant (whose name alludes to the Cubist painter and art-critic, Amédée Ozenfant) would therefore agree with Graves's modernist contempt for sun-worship:

> Apollo the Organizer, [...] seated on Zeus's throne, is beginning to find his ministers obstructive, his courtiers boring, his regalia tawdry, his quasi-royal responsibilities irksome, and the system of government breaking down from over-organization. (Graves 1952: 475)

Lanark's real interest, though, is not in the nearest stellar object, but is instead in the "son", his own son, Sandy, to whom Rima gives birth after she and Lanark leave the Institute together. Lanark's relationship with his son provides an avenue for the tenderness and intimacy proscribed by the masculine roles of his culture: "The small compact body was warm and comforting and gave such a pleasant feeling of peace that Lanark wondered uneasily if this was a right thing for a father to feel" (Gray 1987: 424). This scene opens up a genuine alternative to the ethic which drove Thaw to create his private religion. Instead of an authoritarian relationship between father and son, there is presented a mutually loving relationship in which both individuals may find satisfaction. Lanark, however, cannot properly see the value of this relationship because he is still too infected with Gravesian doctrines. When he should be looking after Sandy, he meets an alcoholic who advises him on the true nature of women:

> "Women have notions and feelings like us but they've got tides too, tides that keep floating the bits of a human being together inside them and washing it apart again. They're governed by lunar gravity [...]. How can they follow ordinary notions of decency when they're driven by the moon?" (Gray 1987: 427)

With this excuse, Lanark neglects Sandy in order to get drunk, and acquiesces in a misogynistic indifference: "A warm stupidity began to spread softly through him. He heard the man say, 'You have to like women but not care for them: not care what they do, I mean'" (Gray 1987: 428). Lanark's consequent insensitivity to his loved ones drives Rima away, and she takes Sandy with her.

Lanark is then seduced again by the prospect of being part of a ruling Elite. He abandons his son, and realises what he is losing only when Sandy observes his departure for the Assembly – a kind of United Nations – where he has been invited as a delegate: "the watcher was surely Sandy and at once the grotesque flimsy aircraft and being a delegate and being a provost seemed stupid evasions of the realest thing in the world" (Gray 1987: 467). The highest reality, Lanark understands briefly, is not the divine realm inhabited by moon-goddesses. Instead, the everyday social world, neglected by cultic modernism, should be his primary concern. This anagnorisis, however, comes too late – Lanark will only have again his relationship with Sandy in a dream granted by Nastler, his conjuring author (whom Lanark meets in a seemingly postmodern piece of narratological mischief).

The importance of personal relations is emphasised elsewhere in *Lanark*. Issues of the highest reality, of what in the world is most substantial, are introduced in the Prologue, where the storyteller of the book introduces himself, and explains his own distance from his everyday community. The narrator of *Lanark* is the "Oracle", who is bidden to narrate at the end of the Third Book. To the narratological complications this structure entails (and whether or not they are "postmodern"), I will return in a later chapter. For the moment, it is sufficient to note the effect of a certain kind of rationalisation upon this character. The Oracle "from an early age" is driven by a desire for certainty, for infallible knowledge (Gray 1987: 108). Such certainty is guaranteed by a contact – via reason – with a realm of ultimate being, a place of "main realities" which might exist below our "jangling opinions" (Gray 1987: 108). The most unreliable realm of reality, the Oracle tells us, is what can be "seen and touched" (Gray 1987: 108). In particular, other people are insultingly mutable – they are the most likely to evade our predictions, and the most likely to be a source of disagreement with others: "Compared with his phone number our closest friend is shifty and treacherous" (Gray 1987: 108). The phone number, however, is far more true and certain, "for the number and our idea of it are identical" (Gray 1987: 108).

This guaranteed numerical correspondence between thought and reality propels the Oracle towards a career in finance, first as an accountant, then as a stockbroker. As he gets richer and richer, his interest in the phenomenal world gradually declines. Eventually, it begins to quite literally lose detail and depth. The Oracle's perceptions reduce to a bare functional minimum:

Where I had once seen irrelevant details and colours I saw none at all. Stone, wood and patterned surfaces became plain surfaces. The weaves of cloths were indistinguishable, and all doors look flush-panelled. (Gray 1987: 110)

These perceptions also eventually dwindle and disappear until the Oracle is left alone and disembodied in a featureless grey void. With no future before him, and only his past to reflect upon, he recalls how his restless and uprooted childhood led him to see a "calm and dependable" life as his goal, an ideal chosen because his formative experiences had led him "to dread the body and love numbers" (Gray 1987: 116).

This little fable, of course, parallels Thaw's withdrawal from embodied life, and attempted communion with a higher reality. Where Thaw has the moon goddess, the Oracle has a Platonic realm of numbers. Both narratives, though, tell of an inability to find communion, and of the psychological destruction which ensues. The connection with literary modernism I have already examined. Are there, though, other intertextual parallels, perhaps of a more local kind?

Spiritual communion in Scottish literature

There may seem little in the foregoing reading that is a matter of a distinctively Scottish literary context – unless we count the connection between Frazer and Graves as an instance of "Scottishness". However, there is a vital context of literature which precedes and follows Gray, and which shows substantial analogies with his work. For every element of my reading, there is some predecessor, contemporary, or successor in Scottish literature. What is revealed by this literary environment is a common revulsion towards the theological remnants in everyday Scottish culture, coupled with an equal scepticism towards the transcendental personal relations – the spiritual communion – which might seem to overcome this inheritance. As an alternative to such sacred communion, there is a valorisation and exploration of everyday, material (less "sacrificial") rituals of kinship.

Only a few years after the publication of *Lanark* and *1982 Janine*, another work of Scottish literature echoed their representation of a fatalistic society plagued by a sense of "original sin". The protagonist of Iain Banks's *Espedair Street* (1987) is driven to despair by such a belief system. "Weird" – Daniel Weir – is the former bassist and songwriter from a now-defunct 1970s progressive rock band. His nickname derives from his surname and initial (Weir, D.), and is used because of his ungainly height and appearance. The name "weird" is most appropriate, though, in its original etymological sense as "fate" and "destiny" (*Concise Oxford Dictionary* 1976: 1322). Weird is a latent fatalist who sees cosmic punishment lurking in the shadows. His West of Scotland Catholic culture has given him a sense of original sin, a "dreadful, constant, nagging sensation of wracked responsibility" which "could be accounted for just by being *alive*" (Banks 1988: 13). Music seems to Weird a way out of this sense of pending doom: the theological meaning of Weird's career is clear – despite "my hulking, graceless body", "I could create grace, could *compose* grace, even if I couldn't be graceful myself" (Banks 1988: 212). The sad, unlucky end of his band, though, brings Weird's sense of original sin back to life. Weird sees the deaths of two of his bandmates as the "weird" for his attempts to escape the fate that might conventionally await a young man from Paisley – a life in a car plant, or unemployment. Weird, "the angel of destruction", "had shifted the bad luck on to others, so that they suffered in my place" (Banks 1988: 212).

Robin Jenkins's novel, *Poor Angus* (2000) also explores a fatalistic, latently theological, worldview through the character of Angus McAllister, an expatriate English teacher who has returned to his home, the Scottish island of Flodday, in order to "plan master-pieces, as he had longed dreamed of doing" (Jenkins 2000: 4). In order to make this move, he has left behind in East Asia his married lover Fidelia Gomez and her child, Letty. Angus is aware that this might seem rather unfeeling: Fidelia and her daughter are accordingly now at the mercy of her husband, a Filipino racketeer. Angus suspects, however, that his treatment of Fidelia is not a cruel and avoidable act of his own free will, but a necessary stage in his artistic destiny. Having been suitably inspired by their relationship, he must now produce further masterworks: "Only if he produced masterpieces could such colossal callousness be justified. He had produced one, her portrait. Justification, though, was still far from being achieved" (Jenkins 2000: 28). Another relationship with a woman, however, may not so much inspire Angus, as drag him back into a world where the projected end – his artistic immortality – does not justify the means. This is why he prefers – in an echo of Duncan Thaw – to regard the women around him not as moral agents worthy of respect, but as the heaven-sent material for his compositions. When an ex-lover, Nell, arrives, having fled her husband, and desperate for his help, he sees not a fellow being in distress, but further fuel for his creative fire:

> His artist's mind, never more alert, took note [...] of Nell's sudden tears.
> Poor Nell was not to know that he had not really kissed her but rather whatever goddess it was that inspired painters. (Jenkins 2000: 86)

Angus feels especially threatened by the prospect that "he might want to sleep with Nell. Let that happen and he was doomed as a painter" (Jenkins 2000: 76). This is because Nell is largely immune to superstition. Prolonged exposure to her would weaken Angus's own sense of a higher purpose which guides his life and protects him from the consequences of his wrongdoing and callousness. Normally, though, Angus is confident of his future immortality:

> It wasn't spurious second sight [...] but artistic instinct which whispered to him that this painting would be a masterpiece. He would have joined the immortals. It behoved him therefore to think kindly of all those not similarly exalted. (Jenkins 2000: 85)

Like one of the Calvinist Elect, who have been pre-selected by God for salvation regardless of their deeds, Angus sees himself as having been fated to an inescapable aristic "immortality".

Another pattern of transcendental communion occurs in A.L. Kennedy's story "Original Bliss" (1997). There we find a protagonist, Helen Brindle, disturbed by the loss of companionship previously derived from her religious upbringing:

> she remembered when loneliness had been only an easily remedied misunderstanding of nature, because there had always been Something Else there [...] God. [...]. He'd been her best kind of love. He'd willingly been a companion, a parent, a friend. (Kennedy 1998: 162)

Helen's story, though, is one of gradual desublimation of this need for companionship. She is attracted to a world famous intellectual, Edward Gluck, a relationship which begins with her feeling that "she was close to his mind" (Kennedy 1998: 165). Helen even appreciates the fatalism inherent in her mental communion with him: "Obsessive behaviour would read almost any meaning into even the most random collision of objects and incidents. Chance could be mistaken for Providence" (Kennedy 1998: 165). Helen seeks out Gluck and they begin a relationship which eventually blossoms into love. The latter, however, has his own issues with communion. If

Helen needs to despiritualise her longing for companionship, then Gluck's needs to be rehumanised, for he masturbates compulsively to pornography. Gluck himself identifies this behaviour – which he eventually overcomes – as a thwarted outbreak of the need for another person:

> I was busy building myself into a genius [...] and there was so little space for everything necessary. [...] But then again I have never been devoid of feelings – sexual impulses – I've always had what most people have – the desire to be with someone. I've often wanted love. (Kennedy 1998: 244)

While Banks, Jenkins and Kennedy may be seen as owing something to Gray (the preceding novels come after *Lanark*), there are also Scottish authors to whom Gray is himself indebted. As well as finding ideas of spiritual communion in *The White Goddess*, Gray could also encounter them in the work of established Glaswegian novelists such as George Friel. Friel was born in 1910 to a working-class Glaswegian family, and, after graduating from Glasgow University, worked as a schoolteacher in the same city. Although he published short stories and articles until his death in 1975, he is best remembered for his five post-war novels: *The Bank of Time* (1959), *The Boy Who Wanted Peace* (1964), *Grace and Miss Partridge* (1969), *Mr Alfred MA* (1972), and *An Empty House* (1974). A movement – like Duncan Thaw's – out of and beyond earthly community is frequently represented in Friel's work.

In *Grace and Miss Partridge* (1969), the protagonist shares a meal with a member of her family:

> Tommy Partridge always went to see his sister on Sunday. He would stay for an hour or two and he used to take off his jacket and roll up his sleeves and prepare a meal for them both with a couple of chops or bacon and eggs or sausages and liver he brought with him. (Friel 1999: 260)

Friel portrays these meals as a participation in a common life: "they were happy eating together, recalling old times, sharing each other's sorrows, sharing each other's joys, comrades" (Friel 1999: 329). The motif of a communion meal recurs in the gifts of food with which Miss Partridge hopes to befriend the girls in her tenement. McKay, the narrator of *Grace and Miss Partridge*, recalls that Miss Partridge "never ate sweets herself. She bought them just to give away to her favourites" (Friel 1994: 201–2). Only one child, however – the punningly named Grace Christie – seems interested in these sacraments. Miss Partridge therefore hopes to win the girl's love by inviting her to tea, but the meal is a failure; Miss Partridge finds no "communion" with the child: "the great occasion lacked the atmosphere Miss Partridge had expected it to have; there was no intimacy, no communion, no tender preparation for her confession of love, only a wee girl eating bravely" (Friel 1999: 250).

Friel, in private doggerel verse, acknowledged the influence upon his writing of Frazer's anthropology (see Cameron 1987: 18). In *The Golden Bough*, Frazer describes such ritual meals as a means by which one may strengthen "the moral bonds of hospitality, honour, and good faith among men" (Frazer 1987: 201–2). As I have earlier indicated, however, a fuller examination of ritual meals occurs in the work of William Robertson Smith, who is acknowledged as Frazer's greatest influence (see Ackerman 1987: 58). In his *Lectures on the Religion of the Semites* (1889), Robertson Smith further specifies his analysis of kin relations, and clearly shows that communion rituals need not have a supernatural component:

> if I have eaten the smallest morsel of food with a man, I have nothing further to fear from him; "there is salt between us", and he is bound not only to do me no harm, but to help and defend me as if I were his brother. (Robertson Smith 1894: 269–70)

The "kin" formed by a communion meal is a social group with certain ethical characteristics:

> A kin was a group of persons whose lives were so bound up together, in what must be called a physical unity, that they could be treated as parts of one common life. The members of one kindred looked on themselves as one living whole, a single animated mass of blood, flesh and bones, of which no member could be touched without all the members suffering. (Robertson Smith 1894: 273–74)

Subsequent anthropologists, too, have noted that communion meals are foremost among the rituals which mark entry into a group identity. Arnold van Gennep, for example, in his work, *The Rites of Passage*, argues that "the rite of eating and drinking together [...] is clearly a rite of incorporation [...] and has been called a sacrament of communion" (van Gennep 1960: 29). Incorporation is, of course, a perfectly sane, non-supernatural, metaphor: the group created by the ritual meal is a body of which the socialised individuals are, as it were, limbs – or "members" as we in the West say in a piece of unconscious metaphor.

Friel's Miss Partridge, though, is repulsed by the everyday sexual and alimentary rites of incorporation of which her brother is a constant reminder:

> His arms were hairy, and the anchors and mermaids tattooed on them were to her eyes an ugly emphasis of his masculine coarseness. She wanted to forget the world of matter, to escape from it, to be a disembodied spirit, hearing and seeing and thinking without being subject to the calls of nature, freed from the limitations of the flesh. (Friel 1999: 260)

In another of Friel's novels, *Mr Alfred, MA* (1972), two young lovers, Martha and Graeme, show a similar distaste for intimacy in the corporeal, material world: "they never actually held hands. He made no show of affection in public, nor did she. They despised teenagers who did that. They considered themselves older, more mature" (Friel 1999: 421–22). As the narrative describes further their supposed "maturity", we find a curious mingling of the physical and the philosophical which hints at Graeme and Martha's transcendence of the embodied world. Because Graeme is not allowed to kiss his girlfriend (or even hold her hand), he contents himself with a more spiritual kinship:

> the good teeth behind her unkissed lips made him long to be taken behind them, to enter into her. But it was a yearning for a penetration beyond physical space. So with her complexion. She was so blonde her pure skin gave him the illusion of seeing a transparency more spiritual than epidermal. There too she tempted him to dream of passing through an insubstantial curtain and dissolving himself within her. (Friel 1999: 452)

Deprived of sexual penetration – an act which is both physiologically and anthropologically a "rite of incorporation" – Graeme wants to break through into a spiritual world beyond the material one. The traditional philosophical vocabulary of "substance" and "accident" is readily apparent in this passage: an accident is a dependent being; a thing which exists only in relation to some other, substantial thing (see de Wulf c.1907: §62). The implication in the case of Martha and Graeme is that, though they are physically separated, the purity of their love promises a union of their souls in a world beyond sensible reality. The meaning of their bodily separation is inverted by the primary spiritual reality behind the accidental, "insubstantial" world of material things. Indeed, Graeme and Martha eventually kill themselves in an attempt to transcend the material world.

Miss Partridge, however, does return to earthly community. An attempted robbery of her employer's wages allows her a chance to display her commitment to her living fellows:

> She hung on gamely and grimly for death or dear life. She wouldn't let go. [...] It was other folk's wages, girls who worked in sweat and steam, machine-minders, pressers and folders and parcellers, vanmen and vanboys, her own earned share and the manager's salary. (Friel 1999: 361)

With this renewal of an earthly solidarity, her eventual rescue is a secularised ascension – or, rather, a descent to the material world:

> With glazed eyes she saw them come, ministering angels all in white flying on wings of mercy to bear her up in their hands, blonde Sarah Finn bending over her blue-eyed and ramstam behind her Jean and Jess and all the other seraphim, hands reverently clasped at her suffering, praying for her, with others winging forward to raise her from her fallen state to be rewarded for ever in heaven for doing her duty even unto death. (Friel 1999: 363)

Miss Partridge's loyalty to the wage-bag is highly significant: "The wee woman was on guard at once, hugging her bag like a babe at her breast" (Friel 1999: 361). As I have already shown, the act of suckling is for Robertson Smith the primal form of communion:

> The suckling draws his nourishment directly from his nurse, and in fact the Arabs sometimes call milk "flesh" [...]. In this way there is a real unity of flesh and blood between foster-mother and foster-child, or between foster brothers [...] The recognition of milk-kinship rather makes for than against the position that all kinship was originally through women; generally speaking the mother and nurse are one, and the bond of birth is confirmed by the continued dependence of the suckling on the nourishment that it draws from the mother's body. (Robertson Smith 1907: 176)

The communion patterns in the fiction of Gray, Banks, Jenkins, Kennedy, and Friel can be traced even further back in twentieth-century Scottish literature. They can be seen as elaborations of that "heterocentric" motif identified by Cairns Craig in his reading of Nan Shepherd's *The Quarry Wood* (1928). It is possible to see the central character, Martha, as something of a precursor to Duncan Thaw: we are told how "her inner life was too turbulent, too riotous, and absorbed her energies too much fully to leave much possibility of interest in the external world" (Shepherd 1996: 125), just as for Thaw,

Apparent life was a succession of dull habits in which he did what was asked automatically, only resenting demands to show interest. His energy had withdrawn into imaginary worlds and he had none to waste on reality. (Gray 1987: 157)

The parallel to Thaw is especially marked in Martha's ethereal relation to Luke, a fellow student. As Craig notes, "She is translated out of herself and into a spirituality which has nothing to do with mere earthly affections" (Craig 1999: 87). This fleshless communion is more Luke's idea than Martha's, but his unwillingness to do other than worship her leads to a response in kind. She begins to value their attachment in a transcendentally toned vocabulary:

this secret and impossible love [...] was eternal, set beyond the shadow of alteration in an ideal sphere, one of the concentric spheres of Paradise. It would satisfy her eternally [...] – those far shining, terribly intimate moments of spiritual communion. (Shepherd 1996: 102)

Their love is beyond the mutable corporeal world; even space seems to dwindle as Martha falls into one of her reveries, in which she summons up an image of Luke:

The walls and roof seemed to recede [...] very far off, she could see Luke. There was nothing between him and her and she knew that she could reach him. [...] Her spirit flowed out upon him, encompassing and permeating his. (Shepherd 1996: 104).

As with Friel's lovers Graeme and Martha, there is complicity between this "spiritual communion" and sexual fantasy. Martha's imagination allows Luke a kind of magical presence:

She wanted Luke, his presence, his life, his laughing vitality; and it seemed to her, crouching mute upon the floor with the mood upon her, that reaching him she could draw his very life away and take it for her own. (Shepherd 1996: 126)

This presence is intensified by "clutching" at Luke's image, which seems to be Shepherd's sly allusion to guilty masturbation:

her exultant clutching was followed by an agony of shame. But next time the mood possessed her she clutched again. "He is mine. I can hold him. I can have his life in me." And she felt like a dabbler in black magic, the illicit arts. (Shepherd 1996: 106)

This "illicit art" allows a kind of spiritualised incorporation, instead of the more corporeal way that Martha would prefer to have Luke "in" her. Martha, to her credit, does not succumb to Luke's propensity to ignore their potential sexual attraction. She eventually moves on, and learns the value – as Craig has shown – of more earthly relations to her community. In the final sentences of *The Quarry Wood*, a meal of communion marks Martha's return to her kin:

> The kitched was filled with their clatter, till Emmeline cried, "haud the lang tongues o' ye or I see if ma kettle's bilin'," and made the tea.
> And they all drew in about their chairs and ate. (Shepherd 1996: 210)

The value of such secular "commensal" relationships is exactly what *Lanark* gestures towards by showing the failure of Thaw's sacred communion with the White Goddess. Although Thaw's personal cult begins as a response to his repressive (but latent) national religion, and its sacraments of thrashings and dunkings, it is equally indicted. The religions of original sin and cultic modernism both devalue the everyday world of embodied kin relations (such as that which is briefly glimpsed in Lanark's tenderness towards Sandy). Despite its modishness, then, *Lanark* is a traditional moral fable which repeatedly subverts the myth of the artist or writer as an extra-ordinary, heroic outsider. Thaw's inability to find an earthly community propels him towards his private religion; this isolation from others is repeated in the tale of Lanark, and is prefigured in the Oracle's same solitude. This narrative pattern is enriched not only by consideration of the Scottish literature and anthropology which surrounds Gray's work; it is also, as I shall show in the next chapter, amply elaborated when Gray's work is approached using psychoanalytic ideas developed by thinkers within Scotland.

Chapter Two

The divided self – Alasdair Gray and R.D. Laing

Duncan Thaw in *Lanark* has a transcendent personal relation: he pursues, more or less latently, a cult based around a lunar goddess. I have already shown how this peculiar motif relates to both modernism (specifically, Graves's primitivist theory of poetry) and to a context of Scottish literature and anthropology. Thaw's peculiar psychology extends throughout Gray's fiction, which often depicts characters who feel that their truest existence is in the imagination, and who project fantastic companions. Such a retreat into mental existence, *Lanark* tells us, occurs when relations with real others are felt to be unfulfilling: "I want to be free", cries Lanark (the character), "and freedom is freedom from other people" (Gray 1987: 70).

Yet there is another theme to this book: the way in which the significance of Gray's work is better understood by consideration of his national context. The concept of communion has begun to emerge: Thaw, having cut himself off from a common life with his fellows, pursues a transcendental communion (a holy communion, of sorts) with "the white goddess". Other works of Scottish literature contain a similar interest in personal relations – be they real and embodied (maintained, perhaps, through meals of communion), or spiritual and disembodied (with God, or a higher Platonic realm, for example). I have already hinted at some of the Scottish intellectual context surrounding the literary *topos* of communion – the work of Frazer and Robertson Smith may well have been influential, for example, on Friel. To develop this context further, I will in this chapter discuss the parallels between Gray's work and the theories of the Glaswegian psychoanalyst, R.D. Laing (1927–1989), whom Gray has explicitly acknowledged as an influence.

Laing is a peculiar figure. Although his work has undergone a revival in recent years, he is surprisingly neglected for someone who was world famous in his heyday. During the 1960s and 1970s, R.D. Laing's ideas were part of a countercultural movement which was dubbed "anti-psychiatry". The anti-psychiatrists advanced various criticisms of established psychiatric diagnosis and care. Laing is perhaps best remembered for his use of hallucinogenic drugs during therapy, and for his searing criticism of the potential oppressiveness of Western family structures. However, there is a more subtle element in Laing's ideas that stresses the importance of meaningful communion with others. The importance of finding a common life and establishing social contact is also apparent among less well-known Scottish psychoanalysts – and I will make reference to two of these figures, Ian Suttie (1889–1935) and W.R.D. Fairbairn (1889–1964). The precise genealogical relation between such figures and Gray need not concern us here, for Gray's statement of Laing's influence is but a clue to a reading of his work: regardless of the extent of Gray's conscious imitation or inspiration (which may be quite extensive), Laing's theories provide a rich and stimulating interpretative guide. They help to clarify the obscure psychoanalytic themes which pervade Gray's imagery and character psychology, and they also throw light upon Gray's tendency to parallel his realistic narratives with worlds of bizarre, allegorical fantasy.

From the armoured body to the divided self

I have so far discussed, with particular reference to *Lanark*, how Gray's writing presents characters detached from a suffocating society, and beset by a substitution of imaginary personal relationships for real ones. To offer a psychoanalytic reading of Gray's fiction may therefore seem rather unpromising. Can psychoanalytic theory really deal with such issues? After all, psychoanalysis is typically associated with a "decentring" of the human subject: the human pretension to rational autonomy is undercut by the evidence of slips of the tongue, "unintended" yet gratifying actions, and a whole host of compulsive behaviours swept under the carpet by various defence mechanisms. Behind all these symptoms lurk the instinctual energies with which the ego must always unsuccessfully grapple. The work of Lacan and his successors intensifies the Freudian decentring. Even the "I" itself is argued to be a narcissistic delusion formed by the anxious identification of the infant with its mirror image (or with some other representative of mastery over the body and its rebellious forces). The conceptualisation of personal relations in psychoanalysis may seem particularly distant from my reading of Gray: how can such a theory get a grip on the substitution of imaginary persons for real ones, or the attempt to transcend embodied existence in a search for communion?

Psychoanalysis seems most likely to see "liberation" not as the development of an autonomous personality, but as an acceptance of instinctual drives which are an embarrassment to the modern ideal of personhood. A reading of Gray's work in such terms could easily be offered. The fantastic diseases of the Third Book of *Lanark* are, as Gray remarks in an interview with Mark Axelrod, "metaphors for bad mental states, like the tortures in Dante's *Inferno*" (Axelrod 1995: 109). Lanark himself has "dragonhide", a condition which turns his skin into a hard insulating armour. When he was Thaw, he cared little for friends and family – at best, other people were there to be exploited as part of his glorious destiny. Lanark's illness turns this psychic condition into a fantastic physical metaphor: his armoured skin and crab-like pincer parallel his earlier callousness and cruelty. The list of plagiarisms supplied in the "Epilogue" to *Lanark* seems to explain psychoanalytically this metaphor: "the dragonhide which infects the first six chapters [of Book Three] is a Difplag [i.e. a 'diffuse plagiarism'] of the muscular constriction Reich calls 'armouring'" (Gray 1987: 496). The "Reich" to whom the "Critic" who writes these glosses refers is the Vienna-educated psychiatrist Wilhelm Reich (1897–1957). Reich developed the Freudian analysis of sexual repression by claiming to discover a precise physiological correlate for that which had previously been revealed only in the words, actions, thoughts and fantasies of the patient. According to Reich, sexual repression creates "armouring", "a negative attitude toward life and sex [...], a pleasure anxiety, which is physiologically anchored in chronic muscular spasms" (Reich 1983: 7). According to Reich, these muscular contractions lead to "a hardening of the character [...], a rigidification or a loss of spontaneity" (Reich 1983: 145) – loss of autonomy is explained by lost contact with instinctual urges. In order to return to a spontaneous life, armour must be removed by the physical release of emotion – prototypically, by orgasm: "Psychic health", insists Reich, "depends upon orgastic potency, i.e., upon the degree to which one can surrender to and experience the climax of excitation in the natural sexual act" (Reich 1983: 6).

This hint in Gray's text has been developed by David Stenhouse, who argues that another of Gray's works, *1982 Janine*, "draws its theme of the connection between sexual and political repression straight from Reich's writings" (Stenhouse 1996: 114). Stenhouse contends that a Reichian reading explains Jock McLeish's sadomasochistic daydreams – these "fantasies fetishize restraint, yet ironically [...] allow full vent to the feelings that he restrains in his 'real' life" (Stenhouse 1996: 116). Jock's vivid and compulsive fantasies, Stenhouse concludes, are frustrated (and consequently aggressive) desires which have acquired the vivacity of perceptions: "A Reichian would see Jock's fantasy as an elaborate fetish which held dammed up sexual energy [...] transformed by repression into an aggressive and sadistic fantasy" (Stenhouse 1996: 119). Jock eventually recovers some hope and some autonomy: a central part of this transformation is the renewal of his ability to shed tears over his personal griefs – a capacity which was beaten out of him, we recall, by his schoolteacher Hislop. In Reichian terms, Jock's eventual liberation is a removal of the armour which has suppressed his instinctual life: "for the first time since he was thirteen Jock is able to cry [...]. The tears release the feelings which have been physically repressed in the body" (Stenhouse 1996: 119).

A Reichian reading of Gray's work certainly seems very promising. To relate Stenhouse's interpretation of *1982 Janine* to the themes of *Lanark* seems fairly straightforward. Lanark consciously uses muscular tension to repress emotion when he is humiliated by the loss of Rima to the villainous Sludden:

[Rima:] "Sludden and I often discuss you, and he thinks you would be a very valuable man if you knew how to release your emotions."
He lay rigid, clenching his fists and teeth in order not to scream. (Gray 1987: 457)

This tactic also appears in the realist narrative of *Lanark* when Thaw represses his frustrated desire for Marjory:

He lay like a corpse, his brain rotten with resentful dreams. [...] He wondered why his thoughts were so full of a girl who had given him so little. The aching emotions gradually became muscular tightness, his limited movement a way of saving breath. (Gray 1987: 293)

Yet to turn immediately to such theoretical resources does Gray's work a disservice. Something lurks in Reich's analysis which more directly relates the motif of "armouring" to Gray's work. Charles Rycroft notes that Reich's obsession with sexual reflexes also smuggles a social perspective into Freudian theory:

Reich's theory of orgasm [...] asserts simultaneously that orgasms are necessary for the physical and mental health of the individual considered as a single entity, and that to fulfill this function orgasms must be experienced in partnership with someone else. (Rycroft 1971: 49)

This is a rather unusual thesis for anyone who holds – as Reich does – to Freudian premises. After all, the primary condition in Freudian theory is one of narcissism; relations to others are gained only as a result of repression through the Oedipal complex. Reich, on the other hand, even as he asks for expression rather than repression, also holds out a vision in which such apparent regression to selfish eroticism is really a means to more satisfying relations with others. Despite Reich's endless talk of physiological "armouring" (and the ludicrous "orgone energy" which he later postulates), a large part of his interest in orgasmic disorder is as the presumed cause of a certain loss of personal contact: "*The orgastically ungratified person*", Reich declares, "*develops an artificial character and a fear of spontaneous, living reactions*" (Reich 1983: 149). Reich analyses faulty sexual reflexes in order to explain

> the double life which people are forced to live. Their exterior attitude, which differs according to their social position, is an artificial formation which is in constant conflict with the true [...] nature of the person and often covers it up only insufficiently. (Reich 1950: 330)

Such artificial, perfunctory or insincere self-expression is the result of "an armor, a rigid shell" (Reich 1950: 342) which explains "the difference between the manifestations of free-flowing, immediate [...] contact and those of secondary, artificial contact relationships" (Reich 1950: 329).

One does not have to look far, within a Scottish context, to find theorisation of a divided self whose relations with others are artificial. In *The Divided Self*, first published in 1960, Gray's fellow Glaswegian, R.D. Laing, describes how an encounter with a divided, "schizoid" personality leaves the impression that one has run into a false, artificial self: "the self is never revealed directly in the individual's expressions and actions, nor does it experience anything spontaneously or immediately. The self's relationship to the other is always at one remove" (Laing 1965: 80). Not only does recourse to Laing provide fascinating insight into the matter and form of Gray's text, it also employs the ideas of someone whom Gray explicitly acknowledges as an influence. John Clay reveals in his biography of Laing that "Gray had been an admirer of Laing's books since they first came out in the 1960s" (Clay 1996: 228). According to Gray, "I found them stimulating because agreeable. When one writer finds a second agreeable it is most certainly because number one has translated number two into number one's terms" (cited in Clay 1996: 228).

Laing's influence is clearly apparent in Gray's work. In *Working Legs: A Two-Act Play for Disabled Performers* (1997), Laingean ideas are conveyed in a drama written for the wheelchair users of the Birds of Paradise theatre company. The central character, Able McMann, lives in a society where the use of one's legs – rather than a wheelchair – is regarded as shockingly deviant: Able is ostracised and unemployed because of his desire to walk, run, and dance. Although he eventually suppresses these so-called "hypermanic" tendencies, and is able to find work and love, he cannot contain his urges indefinitely, and soon ends up unemployed and facing homelessness. In a rage, he wrecks a pub and is arrested by police (in wheelchairs), who beat him unconscious. The story has a "happy" ending: Able is in a coma for seven months; when he awakes he is paralysed from the waist down. He now has no option but to use his wheelchair – unlike the majority of his society, who are able-bodied, but simply do not use their legs. Although the play seems concerned with bodily disability, it shows the influence of R.D. Laing's challenge to conventional social constructions of normality and deviance. The wheelchair-using majority are not physically incapable – rather, they have been socially conditioned not to use their legs. The analogy with the proscription of certain "abnormal" mental states is quite clear.

The Glaswegian poet Tom Leonard has also identified Laing's literary importance and its relevance to his own and Gray's work. The latter's first book, *The Divided Self*, Leonard argues, stands alongside the tradition of European existentialism found in "Kierkegaard's *Either-Or*, Beckett's novels, Sartre's *Nausea*, Robbe-Grillet, Gabriel Marcel's *Being and Having*" (Mullan 1997: 90). Laing also, though, fits into a domestic tradition which includes Gray's writing: "you can think about Laing in relation to Robert Owen's New Lanark [a nineteenth-century model community], to Alasdair Gray's *Lanark*, to [the artist] Ian Hamilton Finlay's garden at Stonypath", and also to James Thomson's long poem "*The City of Dreadful Night*" (Mullan 1997: 91). In Leonard's opinion,

What Laing got to the heart of was the nature of complicity in relationships within institutional structures, and the creation of supposedly self-invalidating "otherness" in people who do not "speak the right language". (Mullan 1997: 90)

Leonard sees a parallel with his own work, which uses a spelling that attempts to convey working-class Scots pronunciation. This is part of his deliberate strategy to highlight the assumed naturalness of the English spoken by the upper-middle classes in the South of

England, and the supposedly obvious deviance of speakers who depart from this dialect. As Leonard explains,

> the dialect speaker tends to appear in a narrative like Laing's patient in a hospital: there is complicity between author and reader that the speaker is "other", that the user of such language cannot be the person who has written or who is reading the work. (Mullan 1997: 90)

Gray uses a similar tactic in *Something Leather*, though with a subtle twist. The standard spelling is treated as Scottish English, while Received Pronunciation is given a "deviant" spelling. So, for example, the headmistress of an elite girls' school sounds – or looks – like this as she discusses one of her charges:

> "How can we help paw Harriet, Linda? The other gels avoid ha because she does nothing but frown when they speak to ha. The tyootas a lucky if she ansas them with moa than a monosyllable and so am I. The only thing she does in the gym is stretch haself for ouas on the wallbaas." (Gray 1990: 29)

Nor is Laing's influence limited to his fellow Glaswegians. His ideas also seem to have influenced the work of the Scottish author, Naomi Mitchison (1897–1999). Laingian echoes appear in Mitchison's *Memoirs of a Spacewoman*, which was published in 1962, only a couple of years after *The Divided Self*. The heroine, Mary, is an expert in establishing communication with alien cultures. Her work brings her into contact with the centipede-like Epsilons (the "Epsies"), who are "only intelligent" with none of the "lovable qualities" which appeal to human sympathies (Mitchison 1985: 33). On the planet which the Epsilons have colonised live another species, the primate-like "Rounds" who are sociable, emotional, and playful. Mary is taken by an Epsilon so that she can study the relationship between the two species. The Rounds are contained in a courtyard, where they are exhibiting a variety of stress behaviours. Mary records:

> The whole thing began to remind me of something I could not place. And then I did. It was a set of photographs which I had seen during my social history course. These were of what used to be called inmates of a mental hospital, a "bin" as they said in those days, into which violently agitated people could be shovelled out of sight. (Mitchison 1985: 40)

As the Rounds are herded out of the courtyard, another element in the allegory is narrated: the Epsilons apply a metal instrument to the heads of the Rounds as they pass through the exit. The instrument has an immediate pacifying effect by inflicting a small nick on the brain. This is, of course, an analogue for lobotomy: "that little nick [...] turned the fighting rebellious Rounds into docile and unanxious entities" (Mitchison 1985: 43). The dead Rounds are then consumed by the Epsies, who are nourished by their "bloodlike liquor", and who use the Rounds' desiccated bodies as "building material" (Mitchison 1985: 42). The idea (obviously implied by Mitchison's text) that modern culture deadens authentic emotional life is also found in Laing's work. This is especially so in Laing's later writings, where the madman is regarded (over-romantically), as someone who is cast-out for refusing to "fit in", or "play the game". Therapy – including lobotomy – then becomes one more tactic whereby authentic human life may be devoured by the system of modern society:

> We like the food served up elegantly before us: we do not want to know about the animal factories, the slaughterhouses, and what goes on in the kitchen. Our own cities are our own animal factories; families, schools, churches are the slaughterhouses of our children; colleges and other places are the kitchens. As adults in marriages and business, we eat the product. (Laing 1971: 101)

Plenty of evidence exists for Laing's importance within contemporary Scottish literature. But although Gray speaks of having "translated" Laing's ideas into his own terms, the analysis which I now offer should not be taken to necessarily imply a whole-hearted effort of synthesis and assimilation on Gray's part. Laing's conscious influence on Gray might in fact be limited to a few texts, some word-of-mouth discussion, and a general sense of the man's ideas. On the other hand, Gray may have immersed himself in everything Laing wrote. The actual genealogical relation is hard to determine and not wholly relevant. There may be other explanatory factors why Laingean motifs recur in Gray's work. For example, there are thinkers who have inspired Gray – such as Reich – to whom a Laingean analysis may be profitably applied because of a similarity in ideas. Indeed, Laing's ideas may be set against Gray's texts without even a distant conscious relation being implied. Even if Gray had never heard of Laing in his life, a profitable reading still occurs when a hypothetical dialogue is created between Gray's literature and Laing's theories.

Perhaps the greatest obstacle to such a dialogue is the present lamentable obscurity of Laing's ideas within literary criticism. This is unfortunate because Laing is the most literary of psychoanalysts. He explicitly states at several points in his career that his brand of psychiatry is akin to literary or scriptural interpretation. The psychiatrist is an exegete, and the patient is a baffling and puzzling text. With skill and empathy, the psychiatrist can develop the elasticity to transpose himself into the other's worldview, just as the interpreter of a text can enter into a historically or geographically alien culture (or as Mitchison's spacewoman can empathise with interplanetary alien life). Laing tells his readers,

> The personalities of doctor and psychotic, no less than the personalities of expositor and author, do not stand opposed to each other as two external facts that do not meet and cannot be compared. Like the expositor the therapist must have the plasticity to transpose himself into another strange and even alien view of the world. In this act, he draws on his own psychotic possibilities, without forgoing his sanity. (Laing 1965: 34)

Laing's work, however, is puzzling to many Freudian-minded literary critics precisely because Laing, though he is an interpreter, refuses to engage in psychoanalytic "interpretation". Laing regarded this procedure as an effort to reduce the plurality of human experience to a single unifying model. Freudian theory, with its constant references to the instincts and their vicissitudes, seemed to involve a mistaken mimicry of the natural sciences. At one point in his autobiography, *Wisdom, Madness, and Folly*, Laing recounts a tale of an elderly man leaving his wife's funeral. The widower turned to the minister and told him, "You know, I've lived with that woman fifty years, and I never liked her" (Laing 1998: 136). This narrative seems to have crystallised Laing's opposition to the wilful imposition of psychoanalytic categories: "It had never occurred to me that some sort of grief and mourning was not the usual response to bereavement. If it did not appear, then I automatically interpreted that as a manic defence" (Laing 1998: 136). By "interpreting" this behaviour as instance of mental illness, Laing would have in fact obstructed any genuine understanding of the man's ambivalent feelings.

As this emphasis on authentic communication suggests, Laing is sensitive to the status of those who are excluded from our communities. He recalls, for example, how rituals of communion seemed to effect a change even amongst chronic mental patients:

> In Gartnavel, in the so-called "back wards", I have seen catatonic patients who hardly make a move, or utter a word, or seem to notice or care about anyone or anything around them year in and year out, smile, laugh, shake hands, wish someone "A Guid New Year" and even dance ... and then by the afternoon or evening or next morning revert to their listless apathy. [...] If any drug had this effect, for a few hours, even minutes, it would be world famous, and would deserve to be celebrated as much as the Scottish New Year. The intoxicant here however

is not a drug, not even alcoholic spirits, but the celebration of a spirit of fellowship. (Laing 1998: 31–32)

Laing therefore often implies that therapy creates a community that recognises the authentic being of the patient:

> This rift or rent [across the sane-mad line] is healed through a relationship with anybody, but it has to be somebody. Any "relationship" through which this factor heals is "therapeutic", whether it is what is called, professionally, a "therapeutic relationship" or not. The loss of a sense of human solidarity and camaraderie and communion affects people in different ways. Some people never seem to miss it. Others can't get on without it. (Laing 1998: 32)

Laing's kind of psychiatry clearly dissents from the instinctual and physiological paradigm relied upon by, for example, Freud and Reich. Yet, as we have seen, Reich's work unwittingly approaches Laing's in at least one aspect: Reich partly wants to restore interpersonal meaning to instinctual gratification. A Laingian reading of Gray's fiction can develop the idea of sexuality as communion, and can eventually supplant a more traditional decentring psychoanalytic reading based on the "instincts". Metaphors – such as dragonhide – which seem so Reichian, may be "translated" back into Laing's intersubjective and interpretative paradigm. In *Interpersonal Perception*, published in 1966, Laing argues that self-consciousness, or "self-perception", is not an immediate given, but is instead a synthesis of one's own self-image with that of others:

> we have ego (self) and alter (other). We recognize that I have my own view of myself (direct perspective) in terms of which I establish my self-identity. However, self-identity is an abstraction.
> We recognize furthermore that ego exists for alter. This gives my being-for-the-other, or one's identity for the other. [...] The other I am for the other is a constant concern of us all. (Laing, Phillipson and Lee 1966: 5)

Indeed, myself-for-me and myself-for-you may involve radically different interpretations of the same actions:

> I act in a way that is *cautious* to me, but *cowardly* to you.
> You act in a way that is *courageous* to you, but *foolhardy* to me. (Laing, Phillipson and Lee 1966: 11)

Laing's interpersonal analysis helps him to account for personalities who are divided into an inner mental life and an alienated outer existence. If a particular social context provides no place for the self to recognise itself in others then a retreat inwards may occur.

If, for example, one's artistic inclinations are dismissed as wasteful, frivolous, unproductive and pretentious, then this inhospitable social context may create a divided "schizoid" self. I have therefore already shown a Laingean parallel in Gray's work: both Jock McLeish and Duncan Thaw grow up in environments where compassion and artistic creativity, respectively, find no welcoming, confirming responses. Gray's novella *The Fall of Kelvin Walker* also develops this motif, and provides clear evidence against a purely Reichean reading. In this tale, the protagonist, Kelvin Walker, renounces his Calvinist religion and leaves his small hometown for London, where he pretends to be the renowned Scottish broadcaster, Hector McKellar. Kelvin is eventually detected by McKellar, who arranges that he be employed as a television interviewer. Kelvin's increasingly political agenda, however, leads McKellar to plant Kelvin's father in the studio audience. The latter humiliates his son on national television over the theft of forty pounds and some jewellery. In *The Fall of Kelvin Walker*, we see again the motif of muscular spasm (and also of original sin) as the protagonist is shamed by his father:

Kelvin [...] compressed himself as nearly into an egg-shape as an angular man could. For a moment Hector McKellar feared this egg might roll off the chair but putting out a probing hand he found it muscularly rigid and perfectly stable. (Gray 1986: 132)

Certainly, this somatic response is linked to the beatings Kelvin received as a child: "He heard his father say that his condition was not new – he had always gone like that after a good thrashing, and always took ten or twelve minutes to recover" (Gray 1986: 134). This Reichian muscular phenomenon is not, however, the essence of Kelvin's problem. Rather, it is a means to maintain some self-confidence in face of his father's withering disdain:

Kelvin had tied his body in a knot for two reasons. One was to shield it from the flaying glance of the studio audience and of those extra millions who were surveying him through the cameras, the other was to protect a precious core of certainty from the shattering contempt of his father. (Gray 1986: 134)

Kelvin's knotted-up body protects his self-identity from the attributions of others; the suppression of instinctual response is a means by which Kelvin can refuse to recognise the hostile and mocking consciousnesses of those who witness his humiliation.

A reading which employs Laing therefore contextualises Reichean muscular spasm as one particular means by which the other may no longer be responded to as a living consciousness. This basic pathology — a depersonalisation of others — is apparent elsewhere in Gray's work. Thaw uses depersonalisation to protect his own inclinations from the stifling atmosphere at his school. He is, for example, interrupted while dreaming up a new story in his maths class, and protects himself by ceasing to attend to others as living beings, instead regarding them as pure sense-data lacking life or significance:

> He stared at the teacher's mouth opening and shutting and wondered why the words coming out could hurt like stones. His ear tried to get free by attending to the purr of a car moving slowly up the street outside and the faint shuffle of Kate Caldwell's feet. (Gray 1987: 154)

Depersonalisation is described by Laing as

> a technique that is universally used as a means of dealing with the other when he becomes too tiresome or disturbing. One no longer allows oneself to be responsive to his feelings and may be prepared to regard him and treat him as though he had no feelings. (Laing 1965: 46)

This refusal to recognise the other, Laing informs us, may become habitual and total:

> one may experience the other as deadening and impoverishing. A person may have come to anticipate that any possible relationship with another will have the latter consequences. Any other is then a threat to his "self". (Laing 1965: 47)

This withdrawal from incessant misrecognition of a "false self" leads, however, to an even more frustrated and inauthentic life which seems increasingly imperilled by relations with others:

> to the schizoid individual every pair of eyes is in a Medusa's head which he feels has power actually to kill or deaden something precariously vital in him. He tries therefore to forestall his own petrification by turning others into stones. (Laing 1965: 76)

Petrification is a refusal of communion. Instead of living spontaneously with others, recognising and responding to their feelings, the divided self merely observes the dealings between the false self and other people: "There is a quasi-it-it interaction instead of an I-thou relationship" (Laing 1965: 82).

Understanding the metaphors of petrification is vital to a proper appreciation of Gray's narratives. The protagonist of *Lanark*, though certainly "armoured" in a Reichian sense, employs this armour to petrify himself and others. Although he shatters Rima's dragon-hide, Lanark eventually fails in his relationship with her because of his fundamental indifference to her personal existence. She tells him: "*No matter how bad things get you will always plod on without caring what other people think or feel*" (Gray 1987: 456). Sludden's subsequent request that Lanark be a delegate to the assembly plays upon the latter's propensity to devalue the everyday world of personal relations:

> An intoxicating excitement began to fill him and he frowned to hide it. He saw himself on a platform, or maybe a pedestal, casting awe over a vast assembly with a few simple, forceful words about truth, justice and brotherhood. (Gray 1987: 460)

Lanark's petrification therefore intensifies: he reflects, "leaders need to be mostly dead. People want solid monuments to cling to, not confused men like themselves. Sludden was wise to send me. *I* can never melt" (Gray 1987: 508). Lanark himself is a solid monument, rather than a vulnerable person, precisely because he has come to regard his embodied life as a dead alienated shell. The means to this depersonalised attitude is Lanark's instinctual repression – as Sludden remarks, "What Rima and I admire in you is your instinctive self-control. That makes you a very, very valuable man" (Gray 1987: 459). But this armouring acts primarily as an insulation from intimate personal relationships: as we have seen, the "excited love of his own importance as a provost and delegate" (Gray 1987: 461) severs Lanark's relationship with his son, Sandy, a bond which he briefly and belatedly understands to be "the realest thing in the world" (Gray 1987: 467).

Although Jock McLeish's life follows a similar pattern to Thaw-Lanark's, he eventually overcomes his petrifying mentality. Jock's greatest failure is the abandonment of his first girlfriend Denny, an action accomplished only by phenomenologically reducing her to the level of the mechanical and inanimate: "She screamed like a steam whistle. I bolted" (Gray 1985a: 291). Soon afterwards, Jock is drawn into his unloving marriage to Helen, an act dependent, as I have shown, upon his submission to Helen's father, a man whose "righteous indignation made him look as solid as granite" (Gray 1985a: 297). Jock's solace (so he believes) in his consequent misery is a life of drunken sado-masochistic fantasy. This existence merely perpetuates his withdrawal from social relations. He flits anonymously from pub to pub:

> When I'm at home at the weekend I make a practice of pubcrawling. I spread my drinking between about twenty pubs, visiting six or seven in a single night but never the same pubs two nights running. In this way nobody gets to know me thoroughly or notices how much I drink. (Gray 1985a: 161)

Jock's eventual drunken encounter with a boy in a grocer's shop begins, however, to rupture his armouring against others:

> The boy took the stolen groceries from my pocket, laid them on the counter and said quietly, "Out of respect for your age and pity for your condition I am taking no steps in this matter. But if I find you doing this again I will inform the police." (Gray 1985a: 173)

Jock initially resists this insight into the reality of his being-for-others. The reader therefore finds him counting out sleeping pills, ready to die rather than to remember this moment of interpersonal contact (or "recognition"):

> he came round the counter and quietly put his hand in my pockets and took out all I had stolen and laid it on the counter and 31, 32, 33, 34, 35, 36, 37, 38, 39, 40, 41, 42, 43, 44, 45, 46, 47, 48, 49, 50 will do the trick. (Gray 1985a: 163–64)

Jock's eventual recovery is certainly, as Stenhouse has noted, an expression of inhibited "affect", or "tension". However, in recovering pity for both himself and others, Jock renews his commitment to interpersonal experience. As Jock reflects before his release from his petrified condition, his life after Denny was an endless effort to escape the recognition of others: "If I stop travelling and stay in one place I will become a recognisable, pitiable ('Out of pity for your condition I will take no action') despicable drunkard" (Gray 1985a: 176) – by refusing to acknowledge the reality of others, Jock could escape confrontation with his own pitiable self as perceived through their eyes.

An interpretation of Gray's work based around Laing therefore understands the fundamental meaning of armouring as an attitude of depersonalisation. Such petrification arises in a stifling social context which motivates the individual to retreat from personal relations. Unlike a Reichian reading, the fundamental concepts of a Laingean interpretation are notions such as authenticity and intersubjectivity; instinctual repression is pathological insofar as it escalates a retreat from communion with others.

Fantasy and communion

Gray's work contains many elements that could be loosely termed "fantastic" – which critical analysis of this term, though, is most fruitful? Kathryn Hume proposes that, instead of thinking of fantasy as a genre, we should distinguish two literary impulses:

> These are *mimesis*, felt as the desire to imitate, to describe events, people, situations, and objects with such verisimilitude that others can share your experience; and *fantasy*, the desire to change givens and alter reality. (Hume, Kathryn 1984: 20)

Ultimately, argues Hume, *"Fantasy is any departure from consensus reality"* (Hume, Kathryn 1984: 21). When psychoanalysis meets literary creation, then departure from consensus reality tends to be reduced to a single model based on the premises of Freudian theory. Whatever the fantastic transformations of a literary work, the underlying motive is assumed to be the same as for a psychic fantasy – namely, the imaginary satisfaction of a frustrated desire. This is the generalisation drawn by Freud in his analysis of dreams, where he concludes that *"when the work of interpretation has been completed, we perceive that a dream is the fulfilment of a wish"* (Freud 1953: 121). This inference grounds the expectation in literary criticism that imaginative creation must represent a desired condition which is in some way tabooed, censored, or forbidden.

Given the premises of traditional Freudian theory, this assumption is problematic for literary critics. Rosemary Jackson faces head-on the conclusion that fantasy as transgressive desire is

> close to Freud's notion of art as compensation, [...] an activity which *sustains* cultural order by making up for a society's lacks. Gothic fiction, for example, tended to buttress a dominant, bourgeois, ideology, by vicarious wish fulfilment through fantasies of incest, rape, murder, parricide, social disorder. Like pornography, it functioned to supply an object of desire, to imagine social and sexual transgression. (Jackson 1981: 174–75)

Such a psycho-analytic reading of fantasy must reduce it to the symbolisation of various shocking and revolting activities – as Jackson concludes, "on a thematic level, [...] fantastic literature is not necessarily subversive" (Jackson 1981: 175). Precisely this problem could beset a psycho-analytic reading of Gray's *1982 Janine*. If fantasy is indeed "vicarious wish fulfilment", then Jock's sadomasochistic fantasies are representative of his forbidden inmost desires. At best, the text could have a forensic value as a study of masculine brutality contained by societal repression. Only fear of punishment (external, or "internal" as conscience) prevents Jock from acting out his coercive sexual fantasies.

A Laingean reading, however, provides an alternative account of fantasy which is more truthful to Gray's fiction. Laing argues that the divided self, no matter how petrified, still fantasises about the acknowledgement of others:

> The self avoids being related directly to real persons but relates itself to itself and to the objects which it itself posits. *The self can relate itself with immediacy to an object which is an object of its own imagination or memory but not to a real person.* (Laing 1965: 86)

"Object" should here be understood as the (needlessly obscure) psychoanalytic term for another person. Consider, says Laing, a patient who

> could never have intercourse with his wife but only with his own image of her. That is, his body had physical relations with her body, but his mental self, while this was going on, could only look at what his body was doing and/or *imagine* himself having intercourse with his wife as an object of his imagination. (Laing 1965: 83)

Laing's theory here provides a psychoanalytic grounding for the motif which I have shown in *Lanark*. The projection of an imaginary other, the need for a spiritual communion, is an act of the schizoid self, which even as it retreats from unfulfilling personal relations craves some kind of acknowledgement and confirmation by others.

The pattern appears even more explicitly, and with clearer psychoanalytic meaning in *Something Leather*. This volume of inter-related tales – "novel" is perhaps the wrong word – presents a narrative similar to that of *1982 Janine*, but splits Jock's story of fall and redemption across two characters: Harry and June. The former acquires a sense of original sin much like Jock's. Her parents expect her to be "as clean, pretty and passive as an expensive doll" (Gray 1990: 23). They enforce this depersonalisation by employing a nurse who, like Jock's teacher Hislop, believes in the physical abuse of children: "The nurse produces this perfect Harry by smacking and nipping her when they are alone together, and not because Harry is bad but in order to stop her becoming bad" (Gray 1990: 23). Like Jock McLeish, Harry loses her sense of autonomy: "[her] face wears an intense frown as if she is trying to remember the exact shape of something stolen from her" (Gray 1990: 23). Nevertheless, Harry's only acknowledgement as a person is through this ritualised punishment: after her nurse is dismissed, we find her "sobbing bitterly at losing the one person in the world she was allowed to depend on" (Gray 1990: 24). This repetition of the themes from *1982 Janine* continues into Harry's school days. Although her teachers are far more compassionate than Jock McLeish's, we find that Harry still desires the only act of recognition which she has known. She begs her schoolfriend Hjordis to beat her:

Harry lies flat [...], head pillowed on arm and turned sideways so they can see her calm, absentminded, no longer frowning face. Hjordis squats beside her, whacking at her bottom with wild windmill flailing of the arms and crying frantically. (Gray 1990: 40)

Like Jock McLeish, Harry subsequently enters a world of imaginary sado-masochistic social relationships: "Hjordis is the centre of Harry's love life. [...] Harry imagines erotic adventures with Hjordis in a shrubbery as big as a jungle at first, but in later years it enlarges to a planet" (Gray 1990: 151). Harry's fantasies end only with the death of the real Hjordis:

Hjordis keeps this dream world working. Harry has not seen or heard of Hjordis for over twenty years. There is no obvious reason for imaginary Hjordis to vanish because the real one dies, but it happens. [...] Harry cannot now imagine anyone who adores or desires her, cannot imagine anything at all. (Gray 1990: 152)

The psychoanalytic relevance of these passages may seem confusing to readers schooled in the Freudian assumptions of the theories typically employed in literary criticism. Where is the critical fuel of the Oedipal complex, repressed instincts, "desire", and so forth? The vital psychoanalytic point to note, however, is the direction of sexuality in *Something Leather* towards other people. Without even the imaginary Hjordis as "object", Harriet's sexuality is a futile and empty libido: "Sometimes she masturbates but it is joyless exercise. She listens to a clear childish voice chanting *Give me somebody. Give me somebody.* It is her own voice" (Gray 1990: 152). Freudian theory and its offshoots typically regard the social direction of sexuality as derivative: only by repression does sexuality come to be gratified through others. This analysis, in which sexual intimacy is a kind of masturbation by proxy, was robustly contested by Scottish psychoanalysts who preceded (and influenced) Laing. The psychoanalyst W.R.D. Fairbairn argues in his essay "A Revised Psychopathology of the Psychoses and Neuroses" that Freudian theories are based upon a failure to recognize that the function of libidinal pleasure is essentially to provide a sign-post to the object [i.e. the person]. According to the conception of erotogenic zones the object is regarded as a sign-post to libidinal pleasure; and the cart is thus placed before the horse. (Fairbairn 1952a: 33)

Fairbairn criticises the Freudian assumption that sexual relations with others are merely a displacement – via repression – of sexual relations with oneself. He is particularly sceptical of the argument that "erotogenic zones" such as the infant's mouth are just a means to instinctual gratification. In his essay, "Schizoid Factors in the Personality", he concludes:

So far as the infant is concerned, the mouth is the chief organ of desire, the chief instrument of activity, the chief medium of satisfaction and frustration, the chief channel of love and hate, and, most important of all, the first means of intimate social contact. The first social relationship established by the individual is that between himself and his mother; and the focus of this relationship is the suckling situation. (Fairbairn 1952b: 10)

Fairbairn is quite clear that this reformulation of psychic "drives" carries with it an opposition to the egoistic assumptions of modern political and social theory. In "A Critical Evaluation of Certain Basic Psychoanalytical Conceptions", he states this opposition to the Hobbesian model of human relationships as derivative, selfish exchanges:

Psychological hedonism for long appeared to the writer to provide an unsatisfactory basis for psychoanalytical theory because it relegates object-relationships [i.e. personal relationships] to a secondary place. Indeed, it involves the implicit assumption that man is not by nature a social animal [...] as Aristotle described him in *Politics* [...], and that, accordingly, social behaviour is an acquired characteristic. (Fairbairn 1994: 131–32)

Social life only requires some kind of contractual explanation when one assumes that sociability is a means to an end. Then one may be driven, like Freud, to explain community and communion via a theory of sexual repression. Freud assumes that our original aim in life is merely the "erotic" gratification obtained from various organs (such as the mouth, anus, skin, and genitals). The Oedipal complex is Freud's account of how this supposed initial state of narcissistic hedonism is overcome. He argues that the father (or symbolic father-representative) interposes between the infant and his indulgent mother (or mother-figure), and demands the mother's love and attention. The child (or male child, at any rate), then overcomes his jealous resentment by identifying with the father, and acquiring a rudimentary adult sexual love in which another person is required for gratification. From this initial identification, argues Freud, flow all the later moral accomplishments of socialised life.

Fairbairn's contemporary, the psychoanalyst Ian Suttie provides a scathing critique of the Freudian account of social existence. Suttie understands quite clearly that Freud regards communion with others as a secondary phenomenon:

> The fundamental question we must ask ourselves is "Is society a spontaneous expression of human nature, or an artifact of force?" Freud unhesitatingly and explicitly states that it is the latter. Society for him is maintained only by the dominance of the "leader" over guilty and frightened "followers", just as social behaviour in the individual is (in his eyes) the outcome of repression by fear. We must of course remember the distinction between suppression by coercion, operating at conscious levels, and repression, which is entirely an unconscious process. In the process of socialization of the group, however, the two mechanisms operate "in parallel" to produce somewhat the same result. (Suttie 1935: 97)

In other words, notes Suttie, Freud believes that "the goal of life is self-assertion and self-seeking, limited only by fear of unpleasant consequences or retaliation" (Suttie 1935: 49); unfortunately, in trying to square this premise with the existence of love, tenderness, and altruism, Freud produces a mare's nest of "supplementary theories and explanations which pile conjecture upon hypothesis" (Suttie 1935: 33). Like Fairbairn, Suttie see the solution as obvious: we should just admit that social relations are an essential part of human life, and an end in themselves. This requires a new understanding of the meaning of instinctual gratification: "the emotions borrow, as it were, the *use* of organs [...] and turn them temporarily to purposes that are definitely social" (Suttie 1935: 68). He concludes: "It would be as absurd to regard the sex act as having a selfish 'detensioning', evacuatory motive as to say that a woman desires maternity for the drainage of her mammary glands" (Suttie 1935: 72). To Suttie, the child's communion with the mother through suckling is a prototype of all the social relations borne upon instinctual media – up to and including adult sexuality. Indeed, the real repression apparent in our culture is not sexual, says Suttie. Instead, we repress the non-sexual media of "tenderness" – the stroking and handholding and so forth (including, for Suttie, meals of communion) that mark contact between intimates. So strong is this "taboo on tenderness" that we even assume that such behaviour is itself a substitute for sexual desire.

Knowledge of Fairbairn and Suttie may perhaps allow us fresh eyes to see Gray's texts. Consider the gratification which Jock finds with his first girlfriend, Denny: "We undressed and got into bed and cuddled for an hour or two. Nobody ever had a skin which was smoother and sleeker than Denny's"; "Sometimes I said, 'Are you tired of this yet?' and she said, 'No, not yet'" (Gray 1985a: 209). This inexhaustible contact is not a futile echo of repressed instinct; it is simply unselfconscious intimacy. If there is anything which Jock longs for after betraying Denny, then it is a return to this simple tender communion. The critical literature on Gray – such as there is – has difficulty in even perceiving such psychoanalytically rich motifs. This is largely because the main critical theories in use in literary criticism – those of Freud, Lacan, and Jung – obscure the phenomena in question. Yet there is nothing psychoanalytically marginal about the ideas I have introduced. Laing is world famous. Fairbairn's theories (and, to a lesser extent, Suttie's) were immensely influential upon the "object-relations" school of psychoanalysis, which investigates the effects of early personal relationships upon psychic development. The problem lies in the theories adopted by readers of literature, and not in the availability of interesting, well argued, and fruitful psychoanalytic paradigms.

Fantastic realism

So far I have considered the depiction of psychological fantasy in Gray's schizoid characters. But if fantasy may be a yearning for companionship by a schizoid self then what are the implications for artistic creation? Cairns Craig has identified what he sees as a "Calvinist distrust of the imagination" at work in Scottish fiction: "Novelists must [...] write in the consciousness of their own evil, must doubt the very products of the imagination [...] which they create" (Craig 1999: 201). An account of fantasy as the projection of imaginary others seems to identify (and validate) such a tradition. But this may be a rather limited account of artistic creation. After all, in *Something Leather*, Harry's headmistress reminds her, "the highest art is made through intacoss [i.e. intercourse] with all humanity" (Gray 1990: 139). How can this be achieved through an art that seems analogous to the inner life of a divided self? This is the problem apparent in the character of the unnamed Glasgow comedy writer in *Something Leather*:

when we made love I imagined other women *instead* of Donalda, and other men instead of me. I could not ejaculate without imagining [...] a tyrant with a harem of captured brides, a cowboy sheriff with a jail full of deliciously sluttish prostitutes. My book is full of these fancies. (Gray 1990: 196)

The parallels between these fantasies and some of Gray's own writing is all too clear. What is less clear is how Gray's own writing may escape the implication that it too is essentially an act of masturbation.

A response to this problem can be introduced by considering a Laingian comparison to an argument advanced by Jackson. She argues that fantasy may contain

a desire for something excluded from cultural order – more specifically, for all that is in opposition to the capitalist and patriarchal order which has been dominant in Western society over the last two centuries. (Jackson 1981: 176)

In particular, Jackson tells us, "it has been possible to claim for the fantastic a subversive function in attempting to depict a *reversal* of the subject's cultural formation" (Jackson 1981: 177). Though the themes of fantasy may often be reactionary, fantasy in its highest form is a challenge to various presuppositions of Western culture: the "unified, stable 'ego'" and other such "categorical structures" are threatened by "fantastic works where the 'I' is more than one" (Jackson 1981: 176). A reading of Gray's work in Jackson's terms would seize upon, for example, Jock's suicide attempt in *1982 Janine*, where the single narratorial voice fragments into a polyphonous multiplicity: various scenes are described, wild exclamations are made, and a dialogue begins between "Jock" and "God", while the typography splits, re-unites, divides again, and eventually joins together as Jock finally vomits up his sleeping pills and alcohol.

The narratorial voice unifies again; the unified stable ego returns. Is this then a failure in *1982 Janine*? For Jock recovers from his breakdown, and proceeds (he hopes) towards a life in which such categorical structures as selfhood, spontaneity and autonomy will play an important part. Jock concludes "history is what we all make, everywhere, each moment of our lives"; and resolves, "I will work among the people I know; I will not squander myself in fantasies; I will think to a purpose, think harder and drink less" (Gray 1985a: 340). Purposive action, acknowledgement of objective and social realities, and a commitment to shaping the future: these are the benefits of Jock's breakdown. How might we make sense of these without dismissing them as merely oppressive structures of the capitalist and patriarchal order, yet at the same time giving fantasy its due as a factor in their creation?

Jock's process of breakdown and recovery points not to Jackson's Lacanian paradigm, but to another Laingian underpinning for the use of fantasy in Gray's work – the notion of madness as a spiritual journey. To Laing, Jock's fragmented self would not be the destination, but a stage in a journey:

> If the "ego" is broken up, or destroyed (by the insurmountable contradictions of certain life situations, by toxins, chemical changes, etc.), then the person may be exposed to other worlds, "real" in different ways. (Laing 1967: 115)

Psychosis, Laing argued, could be amongst these transformative journeys: because "psychotic experience goes beyond the horizons of our common, that is, our communal sense", "madness need not be all breakdown. It may also be break-through. It is potentially liberation and renewal as well as enslavement and existential death" (Laing 1967: 109, 109–10). This process Laing called "metanoia". Daniel Burston sums up this particular strand of Laing's theories: "Schizophrenia is metanoia, or an interior journey in which the individual attempts to heal the splits in his psyche by regressing to the point in his development prior to the emergence of a false self" (Burston 1996: 238–39).

Laing sees regression as useful because of data from linguistics and anthropology which show how seemingly natural and (God-)given ways of experiencing the world are arbitrary constructions. From the phonetic structure of language, to the demarcation of bodily boundaries, the world is divided up in a variety of ways. In *The Politics of Experience,* Laing notes how such constructions become sacred; we solidify what we are "taught to experience, out of the whole range of possible experience" (Laing 1967: 51). These structures obscure experiences which are anomalous to them. In order to express this loss of openness to the world, Laing distinguishes between "ego" and "self". "The ego is [...] an instrument of adaptation" – in Laing's view, the ego results from the attempt to make "each new recruit to the human race [...] behave and experience in substantially the same way as those who have already got here" (Laing 1967: 57). Because of the effects of socialisation, argues Laing, we have "lost our *selves*" (Laing 1967: 61). We no longer see that our experience has been formed by shared constructions of the given: "once certain fundamental structures of experience are shared, they come to be experienced as objective entities" (Laing 1967: 65).

A motif of selfhood recovered after an ordeal of breakdown appears widely in Gray's writing. Lanark is freed from his dragonhide when he descends to the Institute, a paradoxical establishment dedicated to helping those who suffer from disease, while at the same time sustaining itself with the energies of those who succumb to their condition. Lanark's spell in the Institute has its biographical parallel in the events described in "A Report to the Trustees of the Bellahouston Travelling Scholarship" in *Lean Tales*. After Gray graduated from Glasgow School of Art, he was awarded this scholarship, and began a disastrous trip through Spain and France. He was regularly disabled by asthma, and "eventually spent two days in Spain and saw nothing of interest" (Gray 1985b: 181). Most of his time was spent in hospital (in scenes reminiscent of Lanark's spell in the Institute's wards) or in a hostel in Gibraltar. Gray's experience seems to have been one of alienation and return: during his spells of illness, he tells us, "my mind hovered above the person I had been in perfect safety, without affection but with great curiosity" (Gray 1985b: 194). This odd little journey – geographical and spiritual – seems to have given Gray liberating insight into his psychosomatic disorders. He concludes: "I was afraid of losing the habits by which I knew myself, so withdrew into asthma"; this was his response to events rather than acquiring the "maturity gained by new experiences" (Gray 1985b: 207). Such pathological dependence upon unrecognised habit also appears in *1982 Janine*. Jock McLeish's breakdown occurs because he is caught up in routines which he has forgotten were once the product of his own active choices. He is imprisoned within what are described by the voice of "God" during Jock's suicide attempt as "dull habits of a bad job" – these have made Jock a "tool blunted by deliberate stupidity" (Gray 1985a: 184). This metanoiac experience leads Jock to understand what was previously beyond the bounds of his common sense. To attempt suicide, he recognises, was "a typical piece of human daftness, […] a fit of despair because I could no longer stand work that I hate, work that was killing me!" (Gray 1985a: 186).

Unfortunately, Gray, like Laing, overdoes the value and plausibility of metanoia. As Tom Leonard remarks, the liberatory possibility of madness was sometimes espoused by Laing as a necessity:

the approved metaphor of "journey" of breakdown in *The Politics of Experience* I had trouble with. It seemed to me that a vulnerable reader with incipient psychotic symptoms might feel they should just hold on as they were at the beginning of a journey of liberation. (Mullan 1995: 90)

Although Laing recanted (or perhaps just clarified) his most extreme utterances, there is a period when he declares that everyday psychosis is "a grotesque travesty" of what madness could and should be (Laing 1967: 119). He prescribes for us all a genuine madness which entails "the dissolution of the normal ego, that false self competently adjusted to our alienated social reality" in order to achieve "a rebirth, and the eventual re-establishment of a new kind of ego-functioning" (Laing 1967: 119). The romanticising of schizophrenia by Laing seems to have a parallel in Gray's overenthusiasm for the metanoiac narrative motif. This is particularly so with the sadomasochistic action in *Something Leather*. As S.J. Boyd points out, the scenes here are not confined, as those in *1982 Janine*, to the imagination of a character. Here the coercive sex occurs in a fictional portrayal of an objective reality: it is neither kinky fantasy, nor even part of a pornographic alternative world (a "pornotopia" to use Steven Marcus's phrase (see Marcus 1966)). Rather, the narrative makes a kind of testimonial claim to psychological realism. This is worrying for Boyd because of what happens to June at the "climax" of the narrative: she is "chained, beaten, caressed, photographed in stupendously compromising positions, robbed of her possessions, shorn of her hair and tattooed all over her body and face" (Boyd 1991: 121). This experience, observes Boyd with puzzlement and annoyance, is portrayed as a one of "religious rebirth" (Boyd 1991: 121). June's experience may be intended by Gray as something analogous to Jock McLeish's process of disintegration and renewal. The intention, however, does not ensure this reception. June's metanoia is most unconvincing: Boyd concludes,

the suggestion, which seems clearly to be present in *Something Leather*, that forcibly chaining, beating, indecently assaulting, depilating and tattooing a woman might be *doing her a favour* is surely outrageous and dangerous. (Boyd 1991: 122)

The metanoiac model, though, does help to clarify the positive role of fantasy in Gray's work. Psychoanalytic assumptions tend to imply that the fantastic impulse is counterfactually directed – motivated not by a desire to know the world (mimesis), but by praxis, by a desire for alteration so profound that even the "laws" of nature may be modified to satisfy our wishfulness. We therefore tend, when thinking psychoanalytically, to regard fantasy as the substitution of imaginary objects for unachieved or unobtainable aims. This leads to the problem I noted earlier: even an interpersonal psychiatry would still treat imagination as a means to fantasised substitutes (specifically, fantasised personal relations). This might lead to some very rich and plausible readings of the content of Gray's work, but seems to reduce literary creation to psychopathology. However, in the framework advanced by Laing, fantasies – such as those experienced in a psychotic metanoia – may have a different role. Daniel Burston notes that "seen in context, a neurotic's fantasies or a psychotic's delusions may be intelligible as symbolic representations of actual states of affairs" (Burston 1996: 126). Consider once more Laing's example of the married patient who attempts to communicate his schizoid condition: "This patient would have been psychotic, for instance, if, instead of saying that he never had intercourse with his wife 'really', he had insisted that the woman with whom he had intercourse was not his real wife" (Laing 1965: 87) – the man's "real" wife is the mental image that he conjures up during intercourse. Laing provides further instances of the meaning which may be found in the seemingly bizarre statements made by psychiatric patients. For example, "depersonalized patients" may "speak of having murdered their selves". Laing points out that "such statements are usually called delusions, but if they are delusions, they are delusions which contain existential truth" (Laing 1965: 49): by withdrawing their ego boundaries into a purely mental life, depersonalised patients have, in effect, killed their embodied self. Even the everyday psychopathology of dreams can be understood in this way. Laing was once present during discussion of

> a psychotic patient who dreamed of two vertical cliff faces standing opposite one another. A mechanical bird emerged from one cliff face, said "Cuckoo!" three times and disappeared, to be followed immediately by an identical performance on the other cliff. (Burston 1996: 47)

To the annoyance of the patient's analyst, Laing suggested that "the dream might represent the patient's perception of the therapeutic dialogue" (Burston 1996: 47) – "cuckoo", of course, is a colloquial term for insanity.

Fantastic experiences and statements, then, may disclose the world better than everyday discourse – the psychotic is merely unable to recognise that his statements are true not literally, but poetically. As Laing puts it, "the individual expresses the 'existential' truth about himself with the same matter-of-factness that we employ about facts that can be consensually validated in a shared world" (Burston 1996: 87). This model of fantasy fits well with the allegorical characteristics of *Lanark*. The people that Lanark meets are echoes of those he formerly knew in his life as Thaw, and are now afflicted with bizarre yet meaningful diseases. Dragonhide, for example, is a fantastic symbolisation of an obscure subjective reality. As we have seen, it communicates the idea of the schizoid self who "petrifies" both others and himself – a notion far removed from the twentieth-century commonplaces of Freudian (or Reichian) theory. Laing sees "petrification" as one response to an "antithesis between complete loss of being by absorption into the other person (engulfment), and complete aloneness (isolation)" (Laing 1965: 44). Petrification (or dragonhide) is therefore at one pole; the alternative is a parasitical absorption into the other person: "Utter detachment and isolation are regarded as the only alternative to a clam- or vampire-like attachment in which the other person's life-blood is necessary for one's own survival, and yet is a threat to one's survival" (Laing 1965: 53). Two other of Gray's diseases – the leeches, "'using their vitality to steal vitality from others,'" and the sponges, "'hiding behind too many mouths'" (Gray 1987: 54) – present alternative (though equally deficient) responses to the problems of one's existence for the other. For example, one character, Gay, who suffers from "mouths", exists at the other extreme to dragonhide, as an extension of another ego:

she unclenched [her fingers] to show the palm. [...]. A mouth lay on it, grinning sarcastically. It opened and said in a tiny voice, "You're trying to understand things, and that interests me."
    It was Sludden's voice. (Gray 1987: 45)

Laing's work therefore provides a psychoanalytic elaboration of Gray's tendency to present a narrative in a realist mode which is supplemented by a fantasised or fantastic parallel. As Cairns Craig has noted, Gray's work does not often represent imagination as creative freedom (the assumption behind Kathryn Hume's distinction): "'fantasy' repeats in emphatic form the conditions of everyday life" because "escape into an alternative world is an escape leading only to repetition in another dimension" (Craig 1991: 98). Gray's fantastic repetition may involve narration of a seemingly marvellous world where the laws of nature work differently. But it may also take the form of inner-worldly fantasies in the consciousness of a character – this is the case with both Jock McLeish and Duncan Thaw. The latter, for example, is often driven to statements which appear delusive, but which express the reality of society and of his petrified condition: "'Men are pies that bake and eat themselves, and the recipe is hate [...]' [...] he also felt buried up to the armpits in a heap of earth and rocks" (Gray 1987: 188). In this utterance, Thaw cryptically expresses both his armoured schizoid condition and the repressiveness of the social organisation which creates this character type. His "madness" is an attempt to convey an experience and insight beyond the ken of his community.

A similar representational use of fantasy has been noted in *1982 Janine*, again by Cairns Craig. The fantasies which plague the inner life of Jock McLeish are not images of his frustrated desires. Their mimetic function is clearly indicated by Jock's excessive protests, for example, that "Superb", one of his dream women, does not resemble his ex-wife Helen, and that there is no connection between Jock's own mother and the sadistic lesbian "Big Momma". The most important representational fantasy surrounds "Janine", whose plight symbolises Jock's spiritual imprisonment: "the fundamental concealment in Jock's fantasies is that the woman on whom he exercises his imagination is, in fact, himself, translated into an adult continuation of his adolescent storytelling" (Craig 1999: 187). As Jock remarks, his stories are about a

woman [who] is corrupted into enjoying her bondage and trapping others into it. I did not notice that this was the story of my own life. I avoided doing so by insisting on the *femaleness* of the main character. (Gray 1985a: 193–94)

Peculiar though it may sound, there is something realistic about Jock's fantasies: "The sexual fantasy world of Jock's inner consciousness is not, in fact, a retreat from reality or its explanation in an alternative form; it is simply its replication" (Craig 1999: 187) – what seems to Jock to be imaginative freedom is merely an elaborately distorted brooding on his own spiritual imprisonment. As Stephen Bernstein notes, Jock's fantasies stem from the way he has sold himself out to the expectations of his society:

Jock tacitly suggests that he had been forced to prostitute himself throughout adult life. Prostitution and the internal division it implies go on to become central metaphors [...]. For Jock the basic transaction of a body rented out for the pleasure of others encompasses vast areas of personal, class, and institutional behaviour. (Bernstein 1999: 67)

Jock's obsession with prostitution fills his sexual fantasies, and even extends into near delusion – such as his conviction that a prostitute whom he encounters is an aged, alcoholic Denny. This recurrent fantasy does not symbolise some obscure wish in Jock to become a sex-worker. Rather, the fantasy is a repeated attempt by Jock to grasp the subjective reality of his life.

Jock's fantasies also go beyond his personal existence: "if a country is not just a tract of land but a whole people then clearly Scotland has been fucked. *I mean that word in the vulgar sense of misused to give satisfaction or advantage to another*" (Gray 1985a: 136). During the 1992 British general election, Gray wrote a pamphlet, *Why Scots Should Rule Scotland*, in which he argued the case for Scottish independence. The revised edition, published in 1997, elaborates his reasoning. Gray turns to Scottish nationalism because of what he sees as the British Labour Party's failure to consolidate the egalitarianism imposed during World War Two. To communicate his disappointment with post-Thatcher Britain, Gray describes a scene from Frank Capra's motion-picture, *It's a Wonderful Life* (1946), in which Jimmy Stewart's character is shown his home town as it would have been without him:

> It has become a garish Las Vegas glittering with adverts for strip shows and gambling, the streets full of conspicuously wealthy folk in flashy cars beside beggars and a prostitute in whom he recognizes the faces of old school friends and the girl next door – the values of the rich money lender have prevailed. That is how I feel about modern Britain. (Gray 1997: 105)

In *The Politics of Experience*, Laing issues one of his typically provocative statements: "We are", he claims, "all murderers and prostitutes" (Laing 1967: 11). In a literal, legal sense, we are not. But, when put next to Gray's fiction, this claim makes sense. Murder and prostitution are powerful metaphors for the denial of our own possibilities. We depersonalise others – "kill" them, so to speak – as we retreat into our inner lives, leaving our undead bodies to transact with the so-called "real world" of mutual exploitation. In a society where human potential is alienated, and the fact of this alienation removed from rational discourse, the expression of this condition may come across in neurotic or psychotic fantasy.

The "nonliteral truth" of Laingian fantasy recurs in *Poor Things*, which ranks alongside *Lanark* and *1982 Janine* as one of Gray's most successful novels. The motif is represented in the fantastic death and rebirth of Victoria McCandless, MD, as recounted in "Episodes from the Early Life of a Scottish Public Health Officer", a narrative written, we are told, by Archibald McCandless, MD. Gray, the "editor" of *Poor Things*, claims to have found this narrative of the Victorian era, and some other materials, amongst the abandoned records of a defunct firm of Glaswegian solicitors. McCandless tells how he became involved at Glasgow University's medical school with the malformed surgical genius Godwin Baxter, who introduces him to Bella, a woman in her mid-twenties with the mind of a child. Baxter explains that Bella is the resurrected body of a suicide into which he has transplanted a child's brain. The brain, he will later reveal to McCandless, is that of the suicide's own unborn daughter. Bella, who is ignorant of her origins, matures rapidly, maintaining an engagement with McCandless while simultaneously "eloping" with an unscrupulous lawyer, Duncan Wedderburn. Upon Bella's return (disillusioned by the world's realities), she and McCandless marry, despite the interference of General Aubrey Blessington, the husband of Bella's body.

Following McCandless's tale is a sober narrative by Victoria McCandless, wife to Archibald, who insists that McCandless's tale is a fantasy concocted as he lay dying of multiple sclerosis. The facts of her life are, she claims, very different. Her first husband was indeed General Blessington. She left him, however, soon after she met Godwin Baxter, who had been asked to perform a clitoridectomy upon her. Baxter had refused, and so Victoria suspected he might provide a place of refuge. After fleeing to Baxter's home, she fell in love with him, but he refused to marry her. McCandless she accepted as compensation for the loss of Godwin Baxter.

In her narrative, Victoria attempts to account for McCandless's fantasy, and in so doing, turns to a well-established medical and psychological vocabulary of denigration in which "creative inspiration" is reduced to "a mild fever caused by disease" (Gray 1992: 254). Accompanying this reference to biological disturbance of the brain is a form of psychoanalytic explanation in which Victoria draws upon a (Freud-like) propensity to use hydraulic metaphors to characterise emotions: "As locomotive engines are driven by pressurized steam, so the mind of Archibald McCandless was driven by carefully hidden envy" (Gray 1992: 273). This envy, argues Victoria, can be traced to his deprived childhood; her husband's upbringing contrasted with the privileged circumstances enjoyed by herself and Godwin Baxter. Accordingly, she argues, McCandless's narrative is a compensatory fantasy motivated by a repressed resentment of his superiors: "he soothed himself by imagining a world where he and God[win] and I existed in perfect equality" (Gray 1992: 273–74), a world where Victoria and Godwin were both artificial productions created "by the Frankenstein method" (Gray 1992: 274).

Yet, for all the seeming sanity of Victoria's narrative, there is something deficient in the consensus reality which it represents. With the exception of her desire for Godwin Baxter, Victoria finds it hard to love with anything more than universal benevolence. She recalls her attendance upon her dying husband: "I stayed beside him though I could have done more good at other bed-sides. Never mind. I may want company during my own last days, so am glad I did not refuse it to him" (Gray 1992: 255). Victoria later comes to regret her earlier assumption that individual love was merely selfishness. Her two youngest sons fight in World War One, and are killed in the Somme, while her eldest son works as a propagandist for the "Department of Imperial Statistics". Victoria eventually concludes that what led to their blind obedience was an unspoken belief that their own lives were worthless. Because she did not love them as individuals, she reflects, "I did not give them the self-respect to resist that epidemic of self-abasement" (Gray 1992: 307). In an eerie echo of Ian Suttie's diagnosis of the "taboo on tenderness", Victoria advocates more physical contact between parents and children as a way of endowing the latter with self-respect. In a fictional quote provided in Gray's narrative, Victoria reverses the assumption that love is a means to instinctual gratification, and explicitly links tenderness to maternal communion:

[Contraceptives] fix the mind of the users upon the genitals, so distract them from cuddling. Cuddling is like milk. It can, and should, nourish our health from birth to death. Wedding [i.e. intercourse] is the cream of cuddling, the main delight of our middle years (if we are lucky) but it is not different from cuddling. (Gray 1992: 309).

Victoria McCandless and Iain Suttie are kindred spirits. When the former is on trial for allegedly performing abortions, she defends her employment of mentally retarded nurses, on the grounds that "Many people with damaged brains are far more affectionate, if given the chance, than many we classify as 'normal'" (Gray 1992: 311) – so deficient is our ideal of normality, it rigidly screens out "excessive" manifestations of tenderness.

In light of his wife's later insights, McCandless's seemingly deranged narrative comes off better. In her response to his memoirs, Victoria has to admit "My husband practised what I preached": "I, the fearless advocate of homely cuddling and playful teaching, was kept out of the house by my clinical work" (Gray 1992: 252). McCandless's story of his wife's origins may, or may not, be the literal (albeit fictional) truth. However, the idea that his wife was not born until the twenty-sixth year of her life is certainly a figurative truth. Her upbringing in an affection-starved household and her subsequent finishing-school education left her, she admits, "a rich man's domestic toy" (Gray 1992: 258) rather like the passive "doll" to which Harriet is reduced in *Something Leather*. That, as McCandless has it, Victoria should be "born" with the mind of a child after encountering Godwin Baxter is, at worst, a fantastic distortion (or clarification) of consensus reality to better express the reality of her existence. This kind of truth, though, cannot be conveyed in the down-to-earth "mimetic" thought-patterns employed by Victoria. One requires instead an imaginative transfiguration of reality like that employed by her husband. McCandless's overheated imagination (or, perhaps, his faithful account of a bizarre scientific experiment) communicates figuratively those aspects of reality which are overlooked by straightforward realism.

The mimetic, rather than escapist or compensatory, function of McCandless's narrative is emphasised by the central and undecidable dilemma of the book: what is the status of McCandless's narrative within the world of *Poor Things*? Is it a (fictional) fantasy, or a (fictional) reality? As is widely recognised, *Poor Things* "is a model unreliable narrative, a contest between divergent narrators" (Bernstein 1999: 111). The reader is left unable to decide whether McCandless is a deluded fantasist, or if Victoria is attempting to conceal her mysterious origins. The ambiguous status of McCandless's story is more than mere playfulness on Gray's part. *Poor Things* is, to use the vocabulary of Tzvetan Todorov, a species of the truly fantastic. For Todorov, the "fantastic" must involve narration of events which do not seem explicable by the laws of this world. The true fantastic, however, is a period of hesitation between confirmation that these events are indeed supernatural (the "marvellous") or that they are explicable in terms of the real world (the "uncanny" (see Todorov 1973)). In a pure fantastic work, this hesitation is not resolved – the interpretation is undecidable.

There is, no doubt, a "postmodern" reading of the fantastic. One could regard the fantastic effect as one of flickering between equally valid worlds, between two competing fictional realities with no greater claim to mimesis. Like the psychoanalytic distortion of fantasy into wish-fulfilment, such an approach deprives fantasy of its claim to reality. But why should subjective, rather than "objective" mimetic discourse, so readily lose its claim to truth? As Laing points out, our objective discourses tend ultimately to depersonalise the world, and to cast subjective experience as essentially erroneous:

> It is unfortunate that personal and subjective are words so abused as to have no power to convey any genuine act of seeing the other as person (if we mean this we have to revert to "objective"), but imply immediately that one is merging one's own feelings and attitude into one's study of the other in such a way as to distort our perception of him. (Laing 1965: 24–25)

Existential truths (e.g. "my job is killing me") are just as true as statements about the physical world: they have subjective truth, and may be apparent in statements which seem, from an objective point of view, fantastic (I am not, for example, "literally" killed by my job). Our prejudice, though, is that subjectivity distorts the lens of consciousness, an apparatus which is only truthful when it faithfully imitates the objective world. Laing reminds us: "one frequently encounters 'merely' before subjective, whereas it is almost inconceivable to speak of anyone being 'merely' objective" (Laing 1965: 25). The fantastic, however, allows Gray to present subjective experience – the need for love and tenderness, say – with the force of objective truth, but without either forcing it into objectivity (as a marvellous alternative reality), or relegating it to "mere" subjectivity (as if, for example, the existential "nausea" in Sartre's novel of the same name were merely the side-effect of unpasteurised French cheese).

Conclusion

Lanark employs the same fantastic technique as *Poor Things*. We must remember that the narrator of *Lanark* is the Oracle. His narratorial position may indeed be "marvellous" (in Todorov's sense): perhaps he belongs in the world of the Institute, after having erased himself from our reality, and has indeed been summoned to narrate by Lanark. On the other hand, the Oracle's narration may be "uncanny" (again, in Todorov's sense): he wonders if he is in hospital somewhere and is perhaps just dreaming the whole thing up. "Sometimes I think my body is in the world where I abandoned it, lying in bed in some hospital, kept going by infusions into my veins. If so, I have hope of coming alive one day or dying utterly" (Gray 1987: 117). Either reading is possible. The bizarre events which befall Lanark are therefore an instance of the fantastic proper, for we do not know if they are a (fictional) reality, or a (fictional) fantasy.

In Gray's fiction, this means that the Oracle is narrating existential truths *as if* they had force of objective reality. This narrative strategy functions as a reminder that the truth of subjectivity is increasingly outlawed within the consensual reality depicted by more everyday kinds of mimesis. The reader is invited to consider existential realities such as spontaneity, authenticity, and truly altruistic love for others, and the psychic deformations (such as depersonalisation or "dragonhide") which obscure them. Fantasy, in Gray's work, is frequently realism.

Yet, as I have hinted, the presence of fantasy and the fantastic in Gray's work has been taken as evidence of Gray's "postmodernity". A typical postmodern reading might regard *Lanark*, for example, as an attempt to direct our attention to the essential fictionality of the so-called "real" world. Brian McHale, for example, asserts that "as the novel unfolds, our world and the 'other world' mingle with increasing intimacy, hallucinations and fantasies become real, metaphors become literal"; and this he regards as "the outward and visible sign of the collapse of *oniological* boundaries" (McHale 1987: 45). My reading begins now to approach the vexed and complex issue of the relation of Gray's work to concepts such "postmodernism" and "postmodernity".

Chapter Three

Reading and time

In *Postmodern Strategies in Alasdair Gray's* Lanark, Luis de Juan traces a movement in fiction from nineteenth-century realism through twentieth-century modernism, and beyond to postmodernism. In realism, de Juan perceives a preference for the objective world:

the typical narrative method for the nineteenth-century Victorian novel is the third-person, past-tense narrative [...] which seems to be used in order to privilege an almost exclusively referential or representative function of language. (de Juan 2003: 236)

This model of writing, he believes, is one which aims to approach scientific observation. Modernism, on the other hand, progresses to a different use of language in order to express an "inward turn" (de Juan 2003: 238). The movement towards the representation of subjectivity (rather than objectivity) explains the "solid centres of consciousness" in canonical modernist works (de Juan 2003: 238). De Juan is keenly aware of Thaw's modernist use of art as a compensation for an unsatisfying life – as "an act of evasion and retreat from the phenomenal world" (de Juan 2003: 119). *Lanark* then goes beyond modernism – according to de Juan – because Thaw's imaginative replacement world enters a kind of postmodern ontological hesitancy, for "readers are [...] often at pains to differentiate his world of dreams and fantasies from reality" (de Juan 2003: 209). This foreshadows, de Juan argues, a more general postmodern depiction of incompatible, multiple worlds in Books Three and Four.

A challenge to *Lanark*'s position in de Juan's historical description has, however, begun to emerge in my reading. I have shown how much of the fantasy in Gray's work is a way of depicting the force and validity of subjective experience. In my Laingean reading of Gray's work, subjective experience discloses a world with as much validity as the discourses of science and mathematics. "Dragonhide", for example, is not an element in a strictly scientific discourse (despite Reich's attempts to reduce it to muscular spasm); it is a truthful account of personal existence. This insistence in my reading on the reality of personal experience aligns it with twentieth-century existentialism, and the work of philosophers and writers such as Jean-Paul Sartre and Albert Camus.

A connection between existentialism and Gray may seem unlikely. Sartre, after all, is often thought of as a writer who dwells upon the hellishness of other people, and who can find freedom even in Gestapo torture chambers. Camus' protagonist Meursault in *L'Etranger*, meanwhile, expresses his human freedom by shooting an Arab. There seems little in this apparently bleak and misanthropic vision that may relate to Gray's writing. In particular, Sartre's view of human relations as necessarily alienating and antagonistic fits poorly with Gray's portrayal of the human need for communion. However, Gray has cited Sartre (and existentialism more generally) as an influence. In *Why Scots Should Rule Scotland*, he recalls with fondness

the public library, where I discovered William Blake and Heinrich Heine (in translation) and Hogg's *Confessions of a Justified Sinner* and Sartre and Thurber and more wonderful, influential people than I can list here. (Gray 1997: 96)

The text in question was Sartre's first novel, *Nausea*, "which I got from Riddrie public library in the 2 or 3 or 4 years following my getting an adult readers ticket when I was 17 or 18" (Gray pers. comm.). Indeed, Gray found existentialism generally congenial:

Apart from that book, I preferred Camus' *Stranger* & *The Fall* (read later) as existentialist texts. I don't think existentialism is obsolete. As a vision of life it includes the works of Leopardi, Nietzsche, City-of-Dreadful-Night [James] Thomson, Kafka, Céline. And Thomas Hardie [sic]. (Gray pers. comm.)

To properly appreciate the usefulness of existentialism as a hermeneutic guide through Gray, we have to attend to some fundamental affinities. What makes Gray and the existentialists literary kindred is their shared humanism: both prioritise understanding "deviant" human experience (over, say, explaining it away), and both depict human beings as essentially free. It is helpful in this regard to remember that Laing (whose ideas proved so useful in the last chapter) is also philosophically close to Sartre. The latter knew Laing's bestselling *The Divided Self* (1960), and wrote an appreciative foreword to *Reason and Violence* (1964), in which Laing – with a colleague, David Cooper – analysed the political philosophy of Sartre's own *Critique of Dialectical Reason* (1960). Douglas Kirsner quotes from Sartre's foreword to *Reason and Violence* in order to emphasise the joint Sartrean-Laingean perspective on "mental illness" as the action of a free agent, as a praxis which may be understood by a suitably plastic interpreter:

> Like you, I think that we cannot understand psychic troubles *from outside* ... I maintain, like you I believe, mental illness to be the issue that the free organism, in its total unity, invents to live in an unlivable situation. (cited in Mullan 1997: 31)

The connections extend further. Both Laing and Sartre, as Kirsner points out, operate "a distinction between two realms, the human and the non-human" and elaborate "the consequences of treating human beings as though they were objects or things" (Mullan 1997: 31). Instead of reducing the psychiatric patient to the passive victim of a syndrome that can (and should) be explained by a chain of cause and effect, Laing – in the spirit of Sartre – looks for the intelligible agency behind the seemingly unintelligible chaos of a psychotic's words and actions. Laing's therapy therefore tries to restore the patient to freedom, rather than have him or her submit to an inauthentic belief in their own causal determination. In Kirsner's words, "Laing was to psychotics what Freud was to neurotics – he listened to their stories to help to understand their meaning in terms of wishes and intentions, not of organic processes" (Mullan 1997: 33).

A crucial difference between Sartre and Laing, however, is that the latter sees a more fruitful place for human relationships in the restoration of freedom. This difference is particularly clear in their presentations of interpersonal life. In *Being and Nothingness* (1943), Sartre studies the way in which others are disclosed to me. I do not (and cannot) reflectively deduce the existence of others as objects of knowledge. Rather, the Other is given to me in experiences of which a paradigm is shame – "an immediate shudder which runs through me [...] without any discursive preparation":

> shame is not originally a phenomenon of reflection [...] it is in its primary structure shame before somebody. I have just made an awkward or a vulgar gesture [...] now suddenly I raise my head. Somebody was there and has seen me. Suddenly I realize the vulgarity of my gesture, and I am ashamed. (Sartre 1969: 221)

With this example – for "nobody can be vulgar all alone" – begins the study of what I have called "communion", and what Sartre calls "recognition" (Sartre 1969: 222).

Sartre's understanding of recognition (in his early work, at least) is therefore rather different to that of Laing. As the paradigm of shame suggests, the relation of the Other to self is regarded by Sartre as always threatening. Kirsner reminds his readers, "For Sartre the problems of human relationships were not attributable to human history but were inscribed in the nature of being-for-others itself" (Mullan 1997: 37). In Sartre's words, when the Other encounters me, "I grasp the Other's look at the very center of my *act* as the solidification and alienation of my own possibilities" (Sartre 1969: 263). This vocabulary, in which I am separated from an alienated, solidified self, suggests that Sartre's analysis is – to use Laing's terms – "schizoid". Social life does not contain recognition by communion, but only recognition by "shame" – by an experience which can only result in an alienated, "outer" self.

What Kirsner overlooks, however, is the possibility that Laing's ideas on the schizoid withdrawal from communion may have affected Sartre's later writings. Sartre's biography *Words* (1964), for example, forms an intriguing parallel. There are notable comparisons with some of Laing's patients (and many of Gray's characters). Through imaginative literature Sartre finds a world of higher reality and greater vivacity: "Everything took place in my head; an imaginary child, I protected myself through the imagination" (Sartre 1969: 71). He recalls how through books "I had found my religion" (Sartre 1967: 39); "when my mother took me to the Luxembourg Gardens [...] I lent my human body to these lowly regions but my glorious substance never left its perch" (Sartre 1967: 39). In the absence of a peer-group, Sartre may use books to project imaginary others: "Flaubert was a small, cloth bound, odourless creature, dotted with freckles"; "Corneille was a fat man with a gnarled red face and a leather back, who smelt of glue" (Sartre 1967: 42).

Crucially, Sartre's life with others becomes inauthentic, alienated, and unfree. He is a performer whose delight is "to play at being good" as he builds up the role of infant prodigy indicated to him by the adults around him (Sartre 1967: 19). We even find the motif of muscular spasm as the schizoid Sartre is confronted by the recognition of others (which crucially, the young Jean-Paul can experience only as shame). Asked to fill in a questionnaire of his likes and dislike, Sartre takes the opportunity to play his precocious role, and claims that his greatest wish is "to be a soldier and avenge the dead" (Sartre 1967: 69). He is caught out as an impostor, and chided gently that "it's interesting only if you really mean it" (Sartre 1967: 68). Embarrassed, he engages in Laingean petrification (or Reichian armouring, if we prefer Gray's terminology) in order to ward off his shame:

I [...] went and made faces in front of a mirror. When I recall those grimaces today, I realize that they were a form of self-protection. I was guarding myself against the lightning flashes of shame by a barrier of muscle. (Sartre 1967: 69)

By stifling the shame "shuddering" through his body, Sartre can disempower the others who have seen into his deep-seated insincerity, just as Gray's fictional Kelvin Walker builds a "muscularly rigid" armour (Gray 1986: 132) with which to protect "a precious core of certainty from the shattering contempt of his father" (Gray 1986: 134).

While Laing was writing on Sartre in the early 1960s, so Sartre was writing in 1962 a biography which mocked his own schizoid consciousness, and which may have relied tacitly upon categories borrowed from Laing. Sartre's critique of his bookish early existence therefore provides an interesting springboard for a reading of the narratology in Gray's works. As *Words* makes clear, a schizoid life of spiritual communion can be built upon the act of reading. Gray's techniques have often been categorised as "postmodern"; but may they perhaps have some significance closer to the ideas of existentialism? In particular, how does Gray position the act of reading a historical narrative (be it or real or fictional, political or personal) in relation to the emphasis on freedom and agency which underlies the work of Laing and Sartre?

The schizoid self and providence

Sartre is adamant that reading need not be an evasion of freedom and agency. In *What is Literature?* (1948), he provides an account in which "the author writes in order to address himself to the freedom of readers, and he requires it in order to make his work exist" (Sartre 1950: 37). It may seem that we are psychologically passive before a prose fiction as we allow ourselves to be moved by the events represented within. This, Sartre claims, is not so – not, at least, with better literature. Instead, "reading is a free dream": "all feelings which are exacted on the basis of this imaginary belief are like particular modulations of my freedom" (Sartre 1950: 35). But there is also a style of reading in which my freedom is covered over. This is the method of the "critic", for whom reading is a way of avoiding the embodied world of existential anguish. When the critic picks up a book and reads it, he wishes to enter "a whole disembodied world", "an intelligible world" which reduces the everyday seeable, touchable world to "an appearance" (Sartre 1950: 18). Accompanying this ascension to a higher world, is a devaluation of personal relationships, and a projection of imaginary companionship:

> Our critics are Catharists. They don't want to have anything to do with the real world except eat and drink in it, and since it is absolutely necessary to have relations with our fellow-creatures, they have chosen to have them with the defunct [i.e. dead writers]. (Sartre 1950: 19)

The parallel between this model of "critical" reading and the schizoid personality described by Laing (and depicted by Gray) is clear.

The stance of the "critic" comes in for further scrutiny in *Words*, when Sartre focuses on how the act of reading may conceal the freedom of both ourselves and others. The young (and in my reading, schizoid) Sartre finds the process of reading re-assuring because it allows him to treat his own future as if it were past time. He falls for what he calls a "mirage" which attends biographical reading (Sartre 1969: 126). We cannot help but import a past future into our reading of a man's life:

> It is no good putting yourself in the dead man's shoes, pretending to share his passions, his blunders, and his prejudices, reawakening vanished moments of strength, impatience, or apprehension; you cannot help assessing his behaviour in the light of results which he could not foresee and of information which he did not possess, or attributing a particular solemnity to events whose effects marked him later, but which he lived through casually. That is the mirage: the future more real than the present. (Sartre 1969: 125–26)

He therefore delights in reading the childhood scenes in biographies of the famous:

> without ever mentioning the name Rousseau, Bach, or Molière, the author deployed his skill in planting allusions everywhere to their future greatness, recalling casually, by some detail, their most famous works or actions, and arranging his narrative so that you could not grasp the most trivial incident without relating it to subsequent events. (Sartre 1967: 127)

The act of reading is therefore a kind of spiritual communion, in which Sartre ascends to the Godlike perspective of the author in order to perceive the pre-arranged plan which awaits the young Jean-Jacques, Johan Sebastian, Jean Baptiste (and, naturally, the young Jean-Paul):

> These children lived in error: they thought they were acting and speaking fortuitously whereas the true goal of their most trivial remarks was to proclaim their Destiny. The author and I exchanged moving smiles above their heads; I read

the lives of these false mediocrities as God had envisaged them: beginning at the end. (Sartre 1969: 128.)

Time and contingency are removed from these lives: these children are predestined to choose their future paths, and are guaranteed the recognition and applause of future generations.

Sartre therefore ends up living his young life as if he were a character in a pre-written narrative:

> I found myself on the other side of the page, *in the book*: Jean-Paul's childhood was like that of Jean-Jacques and Johan Sebastian, and nothing happened to him that was not for the most part a foreshadowing. (Sartre 1969: 128)

The act of reading therefore fits into the schizoid paradigm which I have developed in my reading of Gray. Deprived of genuine communion and recognition, the young Sartre plays the role of a prodigy. To assure himself that he will be recognised as such, he turns the lived world into a book – "I used this mirage enthusiastically to be sure of guaranteeing my fate" (Sartre 1969: 126). For Jean-Paul, "there is nothing outside of the text" (to use Jacques Derrida's words sarcastically) because he wants his life to be a completed narrative in which fate ensures his eventual recognition as who he takes himself to be. Even if adults outside his family find him irritatingly precocious, or if the schoolmaster thinks his spelling woeful ("my setback did not bother me: I was an infant prodigy who could not spell, that was all" (Sartre 1969: 50)), Jean-Paul can be re-assured by thinking of the future recognition which guarantees his identity: "I paraded before children yet unborn [...]. I saw my death through their eyes; it had taken place, and it was my true self" (Sartre 1969: 129).

The young Sartre perceives his life as directed by a providential order which guarantees his identity, and which will be understood only by those who encounter him in the past tense through his postmortem biography. The future biographer is a kind of God, who presides over the materials of Sartre's life, and shows their order to the reader – who is in turn vouchsafed a glimpse of this transcendent perspective. Such issues of time and providence also apply to Gray's work. A clear instance of providentialism occurs in *The Fall of Kelvin Walker*. Kelvin, whose schizoid nature and muscular armouring I discussed in the previous chapter, has arrived in London and begun his remarkable ascent through the British establishment. He lectures his girlfriend Jill on what this experience has taught him: "did I manage to get all I ever wanted – work, love, fame, money, power and a home of my own – did I manage to get all these in a few weeks through the strength of my own unaided will?" (Gray 1986: 120). Far from it, says Kelvin: his fate has been guaranteed because he is "a mere glove on the hand of He who engendered the hoary frost of heaven and out of Whose womb came ice" (Gray 1986: 120). This God whom Kelvin projects ("the not quite human thing in the room with us" (Gray 1986: 121)) is analogous to Sartre's transcendental biographer who can see a life from beginning to end, "the future more real than the present".

The plot structure of *Lanark* also toys with such providentialism. After Thaw leaves school, he seems destined to enter the library service. As he rails against his fate, he invokes the Judaeo-Christian God, whose providence seems to have arranged this mismatch between Thaw and his social role: he raves ironically, "Things are as finely arranged as they can be in a world of this sort. Praise be to the Maker and Upholder of all things. Yes! Yes! Yes!" (Gray 1987: 210); eventually he concludes "I have no choice but to cooperate with my damnation" (Gray 1987: 211). Thaw's latent White Goddess religion is apparent, predictably, in the symbolism of his outburst:

"I had a wish to be an artist. Was that not mad of me? [...] I had to learn how things and people felt and were made and behaved and how the human body worked and its appearance and proportions in different situations. In fact, I had to eat the bloody moon!" (Gray 1987: 210)

But perhaps his goddess smiles on him after all, for, while waiting to be admitted to the library service, he attends night classes, and his work comes to the attention of the registrar at Glasgow College of Art. He senses that admission and a grant may be on the way, and daydreams of his destiny: "He soared into dreams of elaborate adventure all dimly associated with art" as he takes on his unique world-historical role to confront "some huge and ultimate menace", a threat which "overhung all humanity but only he was fit to encounter it" (Gray 1987: 213). Thaw is indeed inducted into Art School, an outcome which is, as he admits, contingent upon a chain of events that he must regard as essential to his well-being: "If the head librarian hadnae been in America, and my Dad hadnae insisted I go to night classes, and the registrar hadnae been English and liked my work" then Thaw would be unable to declare to his friend Coulter "I'll be doing what I want [...] I'm nearly the luckiest man living here" (Gray 1987: 218). The temptation, of course, is for Thaw (and the readers of *Lanark*) to regard this narrative as evidence, as Sartre puts it, "that the chain of causes conceals an inverse and secret order" (Gray 1987: 126). Co-incidence and choice lead Thaw along a seemingly contingent path to his authentic well-being – just as the events narrated in Sartre's favoured biographies revealed "the future more real than the present" in the lives of young geniuses.

Novels and biographies, then, can present an everyday narrative of divine providence. God's providence – his knowledge of the future – was originally understood as a way of bringing the sinner to an authentic repentance. As Augustine argued, even an apparently good man may suffer seemingly random misfortune if he is yet to come to sincere repentance:

> Though the sufferings are the same, the sufferers remain different. Virtue and vice are not the same, even if they undergo the same torment. [...] The violence which assails good men to test them, to cleanse and purify them, effects in the wicked their condemnation, ruin, and annihilation. (Augustine 1981: 14)

The difference between attrition (a merely prudent regret, motivated by fears of damnation) and contrition (a genuine act of repentance) was eventually generalised, so that seeming contingency guides the individual not merely to an authentic repentance, but to an authentic way of life. The nineteenth-century philosopher, Arthur Schopenhauer, declares, for example, that the link between "the obvious physical contingency of an event and its moral metaphysical necessity" (Schopenhauer 1974: 209) is most apparent in literary narrative, which he seems to regard as if it were, indeed, just history: "If we carefully turn over in our minds many of the scenes of the past, everything therein appears to be as well mapped out as in a really systematically planned novel" (Schopenhauer 1974: 204). Schopenhauer concludes "that a *secret and unintelligible power* guides all the turns and changes of our lives, indeed often contrary to the intentions we had at the time" (Schopenhauer 1974: 209).

The young Sartre was not alone then, as he projected onto reality the structure of a novel, and felt his self-identity (the great man of letters) guaranteed by a fate discernible only by a future biographer who, like God, could see the future in Jean-Paul's present. Thaw and Kelvin Walker also both seem to share this quasi-religious attitude to temporality, in which a secret power (the White Goddess, God) recognises who one is, and arranges a suitable plot-line to bring out this supposed authentic way of life. This overlap between Scottish literature and existential literature is by no means limited to Gray. Cairns Craig has pointed out, for example, how Muriel Spark's *The*

Prime of Miss Jean Brodie (1961) contains a similar consciousness. According to Craig, Spark's text reveals that

> the novel by its very form, replicates the world as envisaged by Calvin, since it presents reality not as an open future in which human beings have choices to make but as a fixed plot over which the author broods like "the God of Calvin", able to see "the beginning and the end". (Craig 1999: 204)

Nor, I would add, were such self-reflexive devices confined in modern Scottish literature to Spark. The narrator of George Friel's *The Boy Who Wanted Peace* (1964) reflects on a plot device whereby a young boy is re-united with his mother when she sees his newspaper advert pleading for her return wrapped around a packet of chips:

> The whole thing was a sheer fluke, a pure accident, a fortuitous concatenation of circumstances. That Enrico had happened to use that page to put round the chips and that she happened to see the ad at all, was the kind of coincidence that happens every day in the real world that God created but is condemned as far-fetched in the work of a novelist, as if God wasn't the greatest novelist of all. (Friel 1999: 110–11)

McKay, the narrator of Friel's *Grace and Miss Partridge*, sees this revelation of providence as the novelist's prime task. Although his novel is based upon a personal history, he must still find the systematic plan that hints at the moral necessity of a chain of events: "using my sources, I've still got to mould the material, give it a shape, make it mean something, seize the essential behind the accidental" (Friel 1999: 376).

At this point, the schizoid attitude to literature begins to assume a political meaning. The reader must also accept a providential vision of world history: if personal futures are predetermined, then so must be the political histories in which they are caught up. Gray in *Why Scots Should Rule Scotland 1997* points out how such a habit of thought removes violence from the past, presenting it as something providentially redeemed, and hence justified, by the present. Take the Norman Conquest, for example. Gray declares,

> The English were taught to be PROUD of having been conquered because – though painful at the time – it gave them a tougher class of managers who, centuries later, led them to thrash the French at Agincourt and seize the British empire. (Gray 1997: 10)

This projection of the present onto the past can then be used to justify complacency before an unforeseen, but providentially patterned, historical future. If we cannot see that Agincourt and the British Empire were "robberies with violence" (Gray 1997: 10), then how can history teach our children that it is "VICIOUS to mass bomb civilians and grounded soldiers in Kuwait and Iraq"?

A similar providentialism appears in *Lanark*, when Lord Monboddo makes his speech at the Assembly. He presents a sweeping review of world history as a series of progressions which justify their bloody antecedents:

> two world wars are fought in thirty years, wars the more bitter because they are between different parts of the same system. It would wrong the slaughtered millions to say these wars did no good. Old machines, old ideas were replaced at unusual speed. Science, business and government quickly became richer than ever before. We must thank the dead for that. (Gray 1997: 543)

Lanark, in the audience, is nearly hypnotised by this appealing vision of timelessness: "He listened open-mouthed, nodding in the pauses. Whenever he understood a sentence it seemed to say everything was inevitable and therefore right" (Gray 1997: 547). The appeal of inevitability also returns, with a direct relation to an uncritical kind of literary criticism, in Gray's short story "Five Letters from an Eastern Empire". The court poet Bohu writes a poem critical of the empire's repressions of the population. However, Gigadib, the "headmaster of modern and classical literature" entirely removes any call in the poem to political action. According to this "critic", the reader finds that the emperor "is presented as a final, competent, all-embracing force, as unarguable as weather, as inevitable as death. This is how all governments should appear to people who are not in them" (Gray 1984a: 112).

As the "headmaster's" interpretation implies, Gray's writing has to grapple with an enormous and almost overwhelming heritage of providentialism in "great literature". For example, in Tolstoy's second epilogue to *War and Peace*, the great realist historical author expresses his revulsion for the notion of meaningless causation. Like the schizoid Jean-Paul, Tolstoy finds comfort in the idea that recognition of one's authentic being is guaranteed by fate:

> If I examine an act I performed a moment ago in approximately the same circumstances as those I am in now, my action appears to me undoubtedly free. But if I examine an act performed a month ago, then, being in different circumstances, I cannot help recognizing that if that act had not been committed much that resulted from it – good, agreeable, and even essential – would not have taken place. If I reflect on an action still more remote, ten years ago or more, then the consequences

of my action are still plainer to me, and I find it hard to imagine what would have happened had that action not been performed. (Tolstoy 1942: 1334)

As a corollary to this personal providentialism, world history also shows a similar pattern of predetermination:

In regard to the migration of the peoples it does not enter any one's head to-day to suppose that the renovation of the European world depended on Attila's caprice. The farther back in history the object of our observation lies, the more doubtful does the freewill of those concerned in the event become, and the more manifest the law of inevitability. (Tolstoy 1942: 1335)

In such a bookish reading of history, as Gray pointed out with regard to the Norman conquest, contingencies must be seen as a necessary condition in an inevitable process of historical development.

Gray's *A History Maker* tackles this narratological temptation to treat the present as if it were the inevitable outcome of a hidden design. This short novel tells of a twenty-first century world in which the invention of "powerplants" has peacefully revolutionised all societies. These devices provide energy, and can synthesise all manner of organic and inorganic materials. Communities are now small, self-sufficient matriarchies which communicate via a global "open intelligence network", while the male population occupy themselves with televised battles fought between rival clans. Like *Poor Things*, *A History Maker* marshalls a variety of fictional sources. The central narrative is a "third person", "omniscient" account of Wat Dryhope, a renowned Scottish warrior who is approached by the mysterious "Delilah Puddock". Delilah is really Meg Mountbenger, a conspirator in a plan to destroy the powerplants using a specially-designed virus with which she infects Wat. The reader learns of Meg's secret agenda in the "Notes explaining Obscurities" following Wat's narrative. These reveal that the seemingly God-like narratorial voice which tells Wat's story is (allegedly) his own in a manuscript left to his mother, Kate. She tells the readers of how the conspiracy is foiled by the matriarchs, who quickly divine Meg's actions, and quarantine both Wat and the infected powerplants. The moral of the tale is of how a man "that nearly brought the matriarchy of early modern time to a bad end" in fact – despite his own ignorance, and the intentions of those around him – "helped it survive, reform, improve" (Gray 1995: xi).

Suspicions may be raised, though, by Kate's immediate comparison of her story with a narrative of imperial improvement, that of "Julius Caesar describing his Gallic wars" (Gray 1995: xi). One of Gray's narratological tactics – the use of an unreliable narrator – helps to further expose the providentialism of Kate's narrative. Her comments on the main narrative are suggestively coupled with the fact that Wat seems to have written about himself in the third person. Is Kate perhaps the author? She is certainly the editor, and one with a particular interest in presenting Wat's story. Kate admits: "If still alive Meg is sixty-three. Should she reappear and deny Wat's story let none believe her. She was always a perverse bitch [...] I never liked her" (Gray 1995: xiii). If Kate is the author, then the key chapter in which Meg seduces and infects Wat is sheer speculation on her part, for there are no other witnesses to these events: Kate admits that "the account of his [i.e. Wat's] doings with Meg Mountbenger in the gruesome fourth chapter are not confirmed by another protagonist" (Gray 1995: xii–xiii). Is Kate merely annotating and editing a biography, or has she fabricated an account with which to vindicate her son? Perhaps it is simple wishful thinking that leads her to conclude that Meg wanted to seduce Wat, but "failing that she infected him against his will" (Gray 1995: 216).

Kate's narrative of Edenic fall (or Samson-like enfeeblement – Meg goes by the alias "Delilah Puddock") is linked into a wider providential story by the epigraph to the novel. A fictional quote from a future archive mocks the unequal distribution of wealth in "pre-modern" times (our time), and concludes that "the rhetoric of plutocratic bosses needed *economics* as the sermons of religious ones needed The Will of God" (Gray 1995: v). Yet the historical narrative which Meg presents for the establishment of the matriarchies is equally dependent upon the hidden hand of economics. Meg can see no reason for dissatisfaction with her "rational Utopia" because in it all material needs have been satisfied: history has therefore ended. This model of history is, of course, Marxist in its assumption that the generation and distribution of a material surplus is the fundamental "motor" of history. The opposition to Meg's quietism appears in the masculine voices in the text, who find that their lives have no meaning, cut off as they are from the maintenance of society, and needed only as "inseminators" (Gray 1995: 205). This dissatisfaction – which should really be to Meg an atavistic remnant of historical time – is articulated by a commander who is given a new role in the post-conspiracy crisis. He reflects that during the early phase of the matriarchy, "our lives were so valueless [...] that we wanted to lose them"(Gray 1995: 211): what the "modern" society did not provide is any possibility for enduring recognition – for this, rather than any material motive, the men engaged in their battles. Naturally, of course, Meg would like to erase such dissenting voices from the historical record – and this is why her narrative excuses Wat, and condemns Meg.

By turning Wat into the passive victim of a conspiracy, Meg unwittingly emphasises the ambiguity of the title *A History Maker*. From the perspective of someone dissatisfied with Meg's utopia, history can be made by action – a contingent future may be moulded in act of historical progress. However, from the perspective of Meg's redemptive present, history can only be made by narration: by showing the chain of causes, intentions, and co-incidences which has brought about the historyless present. Meg's attitude to time is as providential as that of her predecessors who espoused religious and economic ideologies. She is equally at pains to evade real concern about the world. In her history, we return again to the schizoid attitude to temporality, in which all time is treated as time past. This is something that Sartre analyses in his discussion of the "critic" who seeks an imaginary solace in reading:

[Critics] get excited only about classified matters, closed quarrels, stories whose ends are known. They never bet on uncertain issues, and since history has decided for them, [...] since bloody disputes seem futile at distance of two centuries, they can be charmed with balanced periods. (Sartre 1950: 19)

Even the present, full of concerns and opportunities, is treated as a past present, where choices are reduced to an unwitting complicity with a predetermined future.

Involuntary memory: the abolition of time

Gray's novels, then, often subvert providential representations of biography and history. I have shown how some of Gray's characters long for a providential order which might supply the recognition missing in their everyday lives, and how this attitude may then be exploited in providential readings of world and political history. My argument has therefore linked the schizoid personality (as described by Gray, Laing, and Sartre) with a particular kind of narrative order from the tradition of the realist novel. Yet there is also in Gray's work another narratological challenge – this time to a literary temporality endemic in modernism.

Another of Gray's divided selves, Jock McLeish exists isolated and alone; his everyday life has been replaced by imaginary sado-masochistic relationships which intermingle with his fragmented memories. Jock alludes to a literary manifestation of his own peculiar aversion to memory when he remarks on Marcel Proust's *A la recherche du temps perdu* in its historical context:

> I once started the Proust novel about *Time Redeemed* but soon gave up. [...] However, something in the first few pages made a distinct impression. When the hero is an old man he chews a sweet cake of the sort his auntie gave him when he was a wee boy, and because the taste of the cake is exactly the same as in the past he enjoys it just as much. And the million things which happened to him since he first tasted that cake – the aunt's death, a world war which destroyed his home and killed his friends – these are suddenly a slight detour away from and back to a moment which is exactly the same. Eating that cake abolished time for him. (Gray 1985a: 166)

Time is redeemed (in Jock's misremembered title) by being abolished. Just as the realist novel employed a providential redemption, so too the modernist novel has its own timely way of eliminating evil from the world. But how exactly does this redemption work?

Reference to Proust's original is a useful starting point. The text of *Swann's Way* (in C.K. Scott Moncrieff's translation) does indeed suggest Jock's reading. "Marcel's" experience – one of "involuntary memory" – is an elevation above the everyday world. He feels supreme, essential, immortal:

> at once the vicissitudes of life had become indifferent to me, its disasters innocuous, its brevity illusory – this new sensation having had on me the effect which love has of filling me with a precious essence [...]. I had ceased now to feel mediocre, accidental, mortal. (Proust 1922: 58)

All this results as "weary after a dull day with the prospect of a depressing morrow", he sips "a spoonful of the tea in which I had soaked a morsel of the cake" (Proust 1922: 58). Proust's narrator is abruptly seized, plucked from the present, and thrown backwards in time:

> all the flowers in our garden and in M. Swann's park, and the water-lilies [...] and the whole of Combray and of its surroundings, taking their proper shapes and growing solid sprang into being, towns and gardens alike, from my cup of tea. (Proust 1922: 62)

Interestingly, this experience seems to invite a reading in terms of sacred communion. "Marcel" also recalls how his mother would kiss him goodnight: "she bent her loving face down over my bed, and held it out to me like a Host, for an act of Communion in which my lips might drink deeply the sense of her real presence" (Proust 1922: 15). Proust's "remembrance of things past" (to use Scott Moncrieff's translation of the title) is analogous to "anamnesis" (literally, "remembrance") in the Eucharist, whereby – in certain theological interpretations – there is an actual presence of an event in the past.

Through such anamnesis, involuntary memory – as Jock McLeish comments – redeems and abolishes time. Randall Stevenson has noted that involuntary memory allows vivid recollection in which mnemic ideas strike with the force of sensory impressions – as if, indeed, the past were anamnestically present:

Involuntary memory [...] – the kind of association triggered almost automatically by a sound, a smell, a blatter of rain, or an otherwise random sensual experience in the present – does not simply or deliberately *call* to mind some remembered scene or detail. Instead it so suffuses the mind with floods of old sensation that characters are left virtually transformed into earlier versions of themselves. (Stevenson 1992: 89)

Stevenson concludes, quoting Proust himself, that involuntary memory is used "explicitly to create a fiction which 'suppresses the mighty dimension of Time'", one able to "make visible, to intellectualise in a work of art, realities that were outside time" (cited in Stevenson 1992: 87–88). Barbara Bucknall describes the transcendence of temporality which Proust sees as consequent upon this peculiar experience:

The present is permeated by the past, in the influx of involuntary memory, releasing the rememberer as well as his memories. No longer bound to the moment, he realizes that his existence is not limited to the infinitesimal point of the moment. Beneath his superficial self there lies a real continuing, essential self. Not only is this self essential; it is extratemporal, since it belongs neither to the past nor to the present. (Bucknall 1969: 6)

Involuntary memory provides for Proust an everyday experience in which to ground the doctrine that chronological time is merely an illusory ordering with which the soul veils a higher, non-temporal reality.

I have referred already to Schopenhauer's belief that the providential form of the novel was a straightforward imitation of historical realities. This doctrine was part of his wider analysis, in which time itself was merely an illusion which veiled a higher reality. It seems quite likely that Proust's contact with such ideas was through Schopenhauer. As Bucknall notes, "Proust read at least some Schopenhauer in school" and "must have encountered in many other authors, ideas which were either derived from or similar to those of Schopenhauer" (Bucknall 1969: 14):

> Much of the Third Book of *The World as Will and Idea* [...] could provide a striking theoretical basis for Proust's aesthetic claims. For Schopenhauer, the artist by means of a detached, nonutilitarian contemplation, lifts the object contemplated out of flux, out of the categories of space and time, and makes of it, by incorporating it in an art work, something both universal and eternal. (Bucknall 1969: 14)

The idea that time is purely and merely subjective – the doctrine of temporal phenomenalism – was further derived by Schopenhauer from the philosophy of Immanuel Kant. Time (and space), claims Kant, are a subjective construction placed upon an atemporal (and non-spatial) reality:

> the things which we intuit are not in themselves what we intuit them as being, nor their relations so constituted in themselves as they appear to us, and [...] if the subject, or even only the subjective constitution of the senses in general, be removed, the whole constitution and all the relations of objects in space and time, nay space and time themselves would vanish. (Kant 1929: A42)

The senses have the function of aggregating and ordering things as they are in themselves, so that they appear as objects in time and space. Were we to see things properly, however, we would understand that all "times" co-exist at once in a timeless reality.

Proust's protagonist withdraws from the world of the present in order to glimpse the underlying timeless reality of the world. A similar insistence on the reality of involuntary memory occurs in the Scottish modernism of Neil Gunn's *Highland River* (1937). The narrative, which is closely focalised on the main character Kenn, tells us how the protagonist perceives the "the scent of the heath fire": "Involuntarily it evokes immense perspectives in human time; tribes hunting and trekking through lands beyond the horizons of history" (Gunn 1937: 162). This is not ordinary memory, like that explained by the "usual associative excuses", but rather some collective involuntary memory, which evokes a pre-civilised "golden age": "heath smoke is an affair of time; of family or communal life through immense stretches of time" (Gunn 1937: 167). The whiff of heath smoke drags Gunn's protagonist back into a past inhabited by anarchic and peaceful hunter-gatherers just as surely as the taste of the madeleine cake drags Marcel back into France before the Great War.

Gray, however, has less faith in involuntary memory than his French or Scottish antecedents. A better motto for his treatment of the temporality "revealed" by involuntary memory is found in a remark made by Proust's protagonist, who, when confronted by domestic irritations and torments, remarks "I became at once a man, and did what all we grown men do when face to face with suffering and injustice; I preferred not to see them" (Proust 1922: 13). Likewise, the first half of *1982 Janine* concerns Jock's abolition of the time in his life which led to his abandonment of Denny and his marriage to Helen: "The story of *how I went wrong* is called From the Cage to the Trap and describes events which took place in my eighteenth year of life during certain months of 1953" (Gray 1985a: 191). Jock reflects that "these months [...] contain my meanest and most cowardly actions, actions I have been trying to forget ever since" (Gray 1985a: 192); and so he concludes,

I don't want to remember the past [...]. The past is a flowering minefield. All the goodness I have known grows there but grows among explosives which drive shrapnel into my brain whenever I disturb them. (Gray 1985a: 133)

Proust wanted to forget and redeem the high-explosive horrors of World War One; Jock, too, has his own personal analogue to blank out – his surrender to the conformist and utilitarian demands of his culture.

Jock is therefore initially caught up in an abolition of temporality like that represented in Proust's fiction. He uses a variety of techniques to prevent his stream-of-consciousness from developing into an unpleasant narrative train-of-thought. This self-distraction can be clarified if we examine an act of forgetting which occurs during the course of Jock's narration:

I thought I was smart in that suit but no I looked prim and dull which is why I chose GLAMOUR, chose Helen. Liar. Helen chose me oh, I will gnaw the fingers of this hand to the bone.
Ouch
That hurt. Calm down. Where was I? Thinking about rape. (Gray 1985a: 58)

Pain has a powerful capacity to focus the mind on immediate sensation and thereby to stem the flow of mental associations which might otherwise crowd into the mind. Sexual arousal, however, is

Jock's primary way of narrowing experience down to disconnected moments. This is first apparent during his adolescent evenings at home with his mother, which he whiles away in a schizoid reverie:

> My happiest moments were passed with that woman. She kept me indoors but she never interfered with my mind. Between the pages of a book I had a newspaper clipping to carry my thoughts miles and miles away, an advert for *The Outlaw* – MEAN! MOODY! MAGNIFICENT! above a photograph of Jane Russell, her blouse pulled off both shoulders. (Gray 1985a: 19)

Of course, sexual arousal only maintains its fascinating power so long as it does not reach a climax; and this is why Jock would wish never to lose control:

> I am entering Jane Russell the editor Janine Sontag Big Momma Helen forget her forget her and I am at home again. At home again. At home again. No. No. No. No I am not. I am alone. Alone. Alone. I am absolutely alone.
> [...] HELL HELL HELL I lost control, I lost control. (Gray 1985a: 55–56)

Without sexual excitement to mesmerise his mind, Jock's thoughts return to the failure of his own life: "I hate the *thing*, I hate orgasm, I'm lonely afterward" (Gray 1985a: 29). Despite his powers of fantasy, Jock's misery nags at him insistently: "Superb is imaginary. Helen was real. Why can't I keep them apart?" (Gray 1985a: 33). Jock would prefer that they remain separated because "my few nice memories of love with real women conjure up remorse and rage at what I have lost" (Gray 1985a: 37). His unwillingness to discuss his sexual fantasies with a later lover, Sontag, is therefore ironic: "I wanted to keep fantasy and reality firmly separate because surely that is the foundation of all sanity?" (Gray 1985a: 41). Jock, in fact, wishes to keep his fantasies apart from reality so that he might have a secure refuge from the misery of his quotidian existence: "This is splendid. I have never before enjoyed such perfect control. I have abandoned Janine at the exact moment when I nearly got too excited, and I have remembered nobody real except my mother" (Gray 1985a: 28). To enforce this separation of fantasy from reality, Jock reaches for the bottle when memories arise of how Helen's father browbeat him into conformity: "I hated most of all a total stranger old enough to be my father who walked past me with his two sons into the middle of my own room and WHISKY quickquickquickquickquick" (Gray 1985a: 69). Alcohol allows Jock to further fragment his own self-consciousness and to reflect on a life reduced, he anticipates, to disordered moments of real and imagined happiness: "Sip slowly. The parts of this mind are blissfully disconnecting, thoughts separating from memories, memories from fantasies. If I am lucky nothing now will float to my surface but delicious fragments" (Gray 1985a: 69).

This analogue to the delights of involuntary memory is also clear in *Lanark*. On the first night of the general assembly, Lanark gets drunk and has sex with one or more "hostesses". Immediately after the narration of this event, we are given what seems to be an account of Lanark and Sandy walking in the countryside. This scene seems initially to the reader to be an instance of real happiness for Lanark, who declares:

"I am so content that I don't care when contentment ends. I don't care what absurdity, failure, death I am moving toward. Even when your world has lapsed into black nothing, it will have made sense because Sandy once enjoyed it in the sunlight." (Gray 1987: 515)

The ontological status of this experience, however, soon becomes apparent – it is a dream within a fiction: "He plunged across the heather, tripped and fell into darkness. He wrestled awhile with something entangling, then realized it was blankets and sat up" (Gray 1987: 517). This fantastic moment could only appear real if Lanark were to refuse to order his past into a coherent chronological narrative:

His main feeling was of filth, disorder and loss. He had lost someone or something, a secret document, a parent, or his self-respect. The past seemed a muddle of memories without sequence, like a confused pile of old photographs. To sort them out he tried recalling his life from the start. (Gray 1987: 517)

To do so, he must overcome the attractions of a comfortable modernist amnesia: "His thoughts recoiled [...] like fingers from a scalding plate, but he forced them back to it and gradually more recent, more depressing memories came to him" (Gray 1987: 518). This is the same resolution which Jock McLeish makes after his metanoiac recovery: he realises, "I am postponing the moment when I start telling my story in the difficult oldfashioned way, placing events in the order they befell" (Gray 1985a: 192).

Such an anti-modernist and pro-historical agenda puts Gray's writing in a curious position for current critical categories. His work undermines the providential patterns of the realist novel, but also opposes modernist temporal "achrony" (the loss of temporal order). His self-reflexiveness – in allusions to Proust, for example – is not therefore "postmodern", for it ultimately still supports the explanatory power of historical narrative. Jock is required to overcome his modernist abolition of time in order to tell the story that explains his plight – a story which must also refuse the earlier realist providential patterns of secular damnation and salvation.

Gray's Brechtian fiction

In this chapter, I have linked the ideas of communion and the schizoid self to Gray's oft-noted narratological innovations. Gray's schizoid characters, as they retreat from communion with others, enter – like the young Sartre in *Words*, or Proust's "Marcel" – a bookish world. In this alternative reality, providence and involuntary memory seem to reveal that time is essentially Kantian – an illusion imposed by subjectivity upon the atemporal materials of an underlying reality. However appealing this redemptive abolition of time may be, it is quite unacceptable ethically, for it is an invitation to quietism. As Sartre reminds us, for Kant, "temporal unity […] is conferred on the multiplicity of instants by a being who himself escapes temporality" (Sartre 1969: 131). Can we then say that Kant succeeds in his phenomenalist attempt to recover time from "an infinite dust of instants" (Sartre 1969: 133)? Surely not, for if "temporality becomes a simple external and abstract relation between non-temporal substances" then there can be no way in which to "reconstruct it entirely with a-temporal materials" (Sartre 1969: 133): "Either we will implicitly and surreptitiously temporalize the non-temporal; or else if we scrupulously preserve its non-temporality, time will become a pure human illusion, a dream" (Sartre 1969: 133). Sartre is surely correct here: given that what is primarily real is timeless, then "the chronological order is only the confused perception of an order which is logical and eternal" (Sartre 1969: 133). Such a world, remarks Sartre elsewhere, is without a genuine future: "'Man is the future of Man'. That is exactly true. Only, if one took this to mean that the future is laid up in heaven, that God knows what it is, it would be false, for then it would no longer be a future" (Sartre 1948: 34).

Rather than inviting the reader to the threshold of a higher reality (in the manner approved by a Sartrean "critic"), Gray's work therefore exposes and evades the artifice by which literary narrative may imply that everyday temporality is an insubstantial curtain which conceals a timeless world. Like Sartre, Gray is concerned to direct the reader away from the quietist implications which may be found in literary narrative technique. The apparent playfulness of his work is not a delight in postmodern world generation; rather, it is, as Stevenson concludes, an employment of techniques similar to those of Brechtian theatre:

> *Lanark*, in particular, illustrates the paradox that the most transparently, ostentatiously artificial texts may be the ones most likely to redirect their readers' attention upon reality: as Bertolt Brecht showed, an undermining of seductive, secure containment within illusion encourages spectators to take responsibility for reshaping the world beyond the stage. (Stevenson 1991: 60)

The act of reading a novel may contain within it various assumptions about temporality – that biography and history are providential, or that time is "pre-printed" – which are largely unconscious and taken for granted. Such assumptions may, though, be defamiliarised and foregrounded by an alienation effect in the novel.

I shall now show some of the ways in which Gray's fiction, to use Brecht's words, "take[s] a common, recurrent, universally-practised operation and [...] draws attention to it by illuminating its peculiarity" (Brecht 1974: 144). In order to appreciate Gray's approach, I will here focus on two peculiar features of *Lanark*: the "Intercalendrical Zone", and the use of an Oracular narrator. Some of Gerard Genette's narratological concepts will prove particularly useful:

> we will study relations between the time of the story and the (pseudo-) time of the narrative according to what seem to me to be three essential determinations; connections between the temporal *order* of succession of the events in the story and the pseudo-temporal order of their arrangement in the narrative [...]; connections between the variable *duration* of these events or story sections and the pseudo-duration (in fact, length of text) of their telling in the narrative – connections, thus, of *speed* [...]; finally connections of *frequency*, that is (to limit myself to an approximate formulation), relations between the repetitive capacities of the story and those of the narrative. (Genette 1980: 35)

Another of Genette's distinctions is also relevant to my analysis: "I propose [...] to use the word *story* for the signified or narrative content" and "to use the word *narrative* for the signifier, statement, discourse or narrative text itself" (Genette 1980: 27).

When Lanark and Rima leave the Institute on their journey to the city of Unthank, they have to pass through the "Intercalendrical Zone". There, the reader finds narrative peculiarities of order, frequency, and speed presented as if they were on the level of story. In terms of order, Lanark and Rima hear their own conversations before they happen. Narrative anticipation – Genette's "prolepsis" (Genette 1980: 67) – is presented as fictional reality:

> they were passed by footsteps and voices going the opposite way. The voices travelled in clusters of two and three and spoke quietly and indistinctly except for a couple who seemed to be arguing.
> "... a form of life like you or me."
> "... here's ferns and grass. ..." (Gray 1987: 381)

Narrative repetition is also substantialised in Lanark and Rima's world:

> A tall blond girl, wearing a black coat and a knapsack, squatted on the road with her hands over her face. Rima whispered, "Is it me?"
> Lanark nodded, went to the girl and knelt beside her. Rima gave a little hysterical giggle. "Aren't you forgetting? You've done that already". (Gray 1987: 378)

It is, then, in a quite literal, if fictional, sense that Lanark is tempted to live in the past by a temporal slice of Rima (as if, indeed, he were experiencing involuntary memory):

> The upright Rima walked past him, saying coldly, "Stop living in the past."
> "But I can't leave a bit of you sitting on the road like this."
> "All right, drag her along. I suppose helpless women make you feel strong and superior, but you'll find her a bore eventually." (Gray 1987: 378–79)

Variations in narrative speed are also narrated as story. A narrative might briefly summarise the progress of Rima's pregnancy; in the Intercalendrical Zone, she simply does develop at an extraordinary rate:

> Rima stood still and said desperately, "I can't go on. My back hurts, my stomach's swollen, and this coat is far too tight."
> Lanark stared in surprise. The dress had hung loose from her shoulders, but now her stomach was swollen almost to her breasts and the amber velvet was as tight as the skin of a balloon. (Gray 1987: 386)

Furthermore, the varying gradient of each side of the road suggests that the line marks a boundary between different narrative tempos:

> The road seemed to rise steeply for it became difficult to walk fast, so he was surprised to see Rima vanishing into the mist a few paces ahead. With an effort he came beside her. She didn't seem to be running, but her strides covered great distances. (Gray 1987: 376)

The significance of the Intercalendrical Zone should be understood correctly. A critic such as Brian McHale would interpret this section of *Lanark* in terms of a supposed postmodern inclination to foreground the constructedness – or fictionality – of everyday reality. Such a reading is superficial: the Intercalendrical Zone certainly gives a (fictional) substance to fiction – but this is in no way an attempt to replace our everyday world. Rather, when narrative is made into story it becomes fantastic, and we are reminded that narrative time is not lived time; we cannot elide our suffering, nor live and re-live our best moments in the manner of a Proustian narrator. The Intercalendrical Zone is therefore a formally encoded warning against living one's life in terms of the temporality of a novel.

The second feature of *Lanark* to which I turn is another Brechtian alienation of narratological assumptions. In *Lanark*, the protagonist meets his "author" Nastler, who discusses with him the nature of the reality which he inhabits:

[Nastler]: "Everything you have experienced and are experiencing [...] is made of one thing."
"Atoms," said Lanark.
"Some worlds are made of atoms but yours is made of tiny marks marching in neat lines, like armies of insects, across pages and pages and pages of white paper. I say these lines are marching, but that is a metaphor. They are perfectly still. They are lifeless. How can *they* reproduce the movement and noises of the battle of Borodino, the white whale ramming the ship, the fallen angels on the flaming lake?"
"By being read," said Lanark impatiently. (Gray 1987: 484–85)

The author is like an atemporal God; and the reader is like a disembodied spirit whose reading activity brings temporality to Lanark's world: "'I'm like God the Father, you see, [...] and a reader is a Holy Ghost who keeps everything joined together and moving along'" (Gray 1987: 495).

Yet, of course, the "temporality" of a novel is not at all like that of a real world: it lacks a contingent future. The pre-printed text of a novel is analogous to that predetermined future anticipated by the young Sartre, and intuited by Thaw. Nastler is a "conjuror" (Gray 1987: 484), and an "illusionist" (Gray 1987: 494) for, with the reader's co-operation, he creates a world of illusory temporality. The narrative of *Lanark*, however, sabotages the implicit determinism of its pre-printed text by restoring contingency to its ending. This is accomplished by the peculiar order of the books which make up *Lanark*, of which Nastler reminds the reader:

[Nastler:] "When *Lanark* is finished [...] it will be [...] divided into books three, one, two and four."
[Lanark:] "Why not one, two, three and four?"
"I want *Lanark* to be read in one order but eventually thought of in another." (Gray 1987: 483)

What can be learned by thinking of *Lanark* in this different order? The first two books are quite obviously the Oracle's narrative of Thaw's life. Significantly, the narratorial voice of the third book is also that of the Oracle:

Rima asked who was there and a moment after the voice spoke directly into his ear. It was sexless and eager but on an odd unemphatic note, as if its words could never be printed between quotation marks.
It said I am glad you called. (Gray 1987: 104)

The Oracle here refers to himself both in the first person – as "I" – and in the third person – as "the voice" and "it". Thus, the third book extends the oracle's account of what has befallen Thaw and Lanark up until the point at which Lanark asks the Oracle to narrate. In order to appreciate further the continuity of the narratorial voice in *Lanark*, it is useful to refer to Gerard Genette on the temporal relation between the story and the act of narration:

It is [...] necessary, merely from the point of view of temporal position, to differentiate four types of narrating: *subsequent* (the classical position of the past-tense narrative, undoubtedly far and away the most frequent); *prior* (predictive narrative, generally in the future tense, but not prohibited from being conjugated in the present, like Jocabel's dream in *Moyse sauvé*); *simultaneous* (narrative in the present contemporaneous with the actions); and *interpolated* (between the moments of the action). (Genette 1980: 217)

The narratorial voice of *Lanark* is explicitly the voice of an "oracle" – it also narrates predictively. Unless we arbitrarily posit two narrators for *Lanark*, then we must recognise that the Oracle continues to speak beyond the end of Book Three, and purports to tell Lanark of events which have not yet occurred. The words "Lanark opened his eyes and looked thoughtfully round the ward" (Gray 1987: 357), which begin the fourth book, are the Oracle's prior narration, conjugated in the past tense like the other books, of events which are supposed to occur after he has concluded his response to Lanark's inquiry. In a significant sense, then, the events of the fourth book do not happen: they are merely the Oracle's anticipation of what will (or may) occur after he has completed his act of narration. *Lanark*, properly considered, ends not with the protagonist's rather lonely death, but with the ending of a warning addressed to Lanark, who is still in the Institute, and who is still in a position to forestall the events of the fourth book. Lanark's loss of Rima and Sandy, and his failure as a delegate to the Assembly, are therefore possibilities which may not be realised in his fictional future.

This structure gestures towards a future contingency which the novel cannot normally incorporate. Although the text of *Lanark* certainly cannot change, the narrative can be arranged in such a way that the fictional speech-acts of the narrator possess a hypothetical, future reference. Because of this, paradoxical though it may sound, there results in the fourth book of *Lanark* a narrative without an accompanying story. Anyone who wants to know what "really" happens in the fourth book of *Lanark*, is therefore at liberty to append – in speech, writing, or private musings – their own narrative of Lanark's adventures outside of the Institute.

Conclusion

As my comparison with existentialism implies, Gray is essentially a humanist in his attitude to time and history. Even where his fiction is self-conscious ("metafictional"), it is in the service of a modern commitment to (a contingent) historical progress, for it aims to expose and subvert the "naturalness" of a phenomenalist view of time. This agenda in Gray's writing makes it quite unfashionable in contemporary literary criticism, where metafiction is often regarded as the postmodern exposure of a supposed essential similarity between myth and history. Indeed, Gray's humanism has led him to be depicted as a backward pupil in the classroom of postmodern fiction. Alison Lumsden comes close to suggesting this when she discusses the way in which

> Gray's work seems to suggest that, while the vast economic and political structures which form systems of entrapment [...] may be difficult, if not impossible, to challenge, the individual may nevertheless find some kind of freedom *within* these frameworks. (Lumsden 1993: 118)

The end result, argues Lumsden, are some "fairly traditional, classically bourgeois" conclusions (Lumsden 1993: 118). The problem with Lumsden's criticism is that it seems "classically bourgeois" itself since it implies that "vast economic and political structures" are not the result of concerted human agency, but rather confront us as a kind of second natural world with which we cannot negotiate. If such systems are to be changed, it will only be by the agency of free individuals. There is nothing trivial about the "small" existential freedoms which are so often the subject of Gray's work. Only the purest Marxist ideologue believes in the providential inevitability of historical process – that, as Jock McLeish puts is, "his opponents [...] will shortly vanish since they are WRONG and therefore somehow, even now, a thing of the past" (Gray 1985a: 192).

Conclusion

How "post-" is Gray?

Gray's work has often been seen as important because it seems to show Scottish writing finally "catching up" with the Anglo-American mainstream. Instead of a fiction enmired in gritty realism, and obsessed with nationalism, one seems to discover in Gray's work the postmodern credentials required by currently dominant critical schools. Of course, my analysis has implied that such a reading is superficial, and I have often had recourse to unfashionable critical perspectives such as Sartre's existentialism, and the little-known strand of psychiatry which runs through Scottish culture. By way of conclusion, I wish to explicitly relate my reading of Gray's work to two important and influential cultural theories: those of "postmodernism" and "postnationalism". Where does Gray stand in relation to such ideas; and must we dismiss him as backward if he cannot be accommodated by the readings they offer?

How "postmodern" is Gray?

I have mentioned already in this book the postmodern interpretations of Gray's work offered by critics such as Brian McHale, Luis de Juan, and Donald P. Kaczvinsky. Yet Gray himself is sceptical of postmodernist ideas. In the postscript to *Sixteen Occasional Poems 1990–2000*, Gray refers to a conference he attended in the USA where a speaker discussed such issues:

> His energetic speech led to a discussion that said nothing about the links between vision and word and ignored description of an intricate universe and how well or badly we live in it [...]. The chaos theory was mentioned with enthusiasm by one who seemed to think it a liberation from logical constraint instead of a logical way to solve problems. (Gray 2000: 29)

As well as showing scepticism towards philosophical "postmodernity", Gray has also distanced himself from the application of the generic term "postmodernism" to his own writing. Stephen Bernstein quotes Gray on the superficiality of this classification:

one convenient way of dealing with Gray's work is to label it postmodern and analyze it accordingly [...]. Yet Gray's rancor at being called a postmodernist is evident in several places. He complains of "critics – however friendly – who are so interested in what is sometimes called my *ludic* writing [...] that they forget half my writing is not like that". (Bernstein 1999: 29)

Of course, Gray's opinions still leave room for a postmodern interpretation. One cannot take his words as necessarily authoritative. Perhaps as interpreters we might come to know his works better than he does, and to appreciate them as postmodern productions which have escaped his intentions. This is the opinion, for example, of Alison Lumsden:

While Gray himself rejects the application of this term ["postmodern"] to his own work, it seems clear that not only the strategies used in his novels, but also the issues which are raised within them, can be seen to be broadly in tune with those fictional developments which have appeared in the past twenty years and which have been described as postmodernity. (Lumsden 1993: 119)

For Johanna Tiitinen, *A History Maker* is a prime example of Gray's postmodern writing. She detects in it a blurring of the distinction between history and fiction.

I believe Alasdair Gray is, first of all, showing how deeply sceptical he is of historical truths. [...] Kate's notes, for example, contain nonsensical fictional evidence side by side with historical facts. The reader's attention is thus drawn to the way these facts have been chosen to weave a coherent narrative line of history. (Tiitinen 1999: 279)

If historical writing is a process of "weaving" a coherent line of history, then, implies Tiitinen, history is merely myth solidified into "truth": "By confusing our traditional view of history and fiction, Gray demonstrates how, ultimately, the only thing that sets fiction and history apart is their truth claim" (Tiitinen 1999: 277).

The inspiration for Tiitinen is Hayden White's influential study of historiography, *The Content of the Form* (1987). Arguments such as White's seem to contradict widely-held intuitions about the "objectivity of history". Commonsense presupposes that the past is fixed and unalterable. What has already happened is determinate, and it is determined by intelligible relations with previous past events. Historians therefore seem able to claim that what they discover is already "out there", just as scientists might also claim to describe regular processes that have a determinate character which does not depend upon our consciousness. However, according to White, historical explanation is something that is imposed upon reality by a merely subjective desire for order:

> this value attached to narrativity in the representation of real events arises out of a desire to have real events display the coherence, integrity, fullness, and closure of an image of life that is and can only be imaginary. (White 1987: 24)

As evidence for this proposition, White points out that a plurality of competing accounts underlies historiography: "Unless at least two versions of the same set of events can be imagined, there is no reason for the historian to take upon himself the authority of giving the true account of what really happened" (White 1987: 20). Imagine (if I may give an example of my own) that you are asked to account for the increasing emancipation of women in Western Europe during the twentieth century. You could refer to a kind of idealist historical explanation in which feminist political movements succeed because of the rationality of women's claims to equal rights. Perhaps, though, this seems inadequate. What of technical developments such as improved contraception? But even these two kinds of explanation – intellectual and technological – may still seem inadequate. After all, what of the effect of war economies in Western Europe, where women (with the exception of Nazi Germany perhaps), were required to work in previously male industries? What of wider structural economic questions? The capitalist economy, for example, must liberate women from the household in order to expand the supply side of the labour market. Such plurality inspires White's underlying metaphors of "formal" and "material" causation. Upon the events of history – the "matter" – we *impose* the form of narratological concepts. Historical narrative is "the imposition of the structure of a given story type on the events" by which we "give to reality the odor of the ideal" (White 1987: 44, 21). The competing narratives of history seem to expose the arbitrariness of such constructions, implying that reality is an inherently formless clay which we shape as we will. As Johanna Tiitinen puts its, the historian is like "the map maker in Jorge Luis Borges's story [who] saw his map taking the shape of his own face" (Tiitinen 1999: 280).

White, though, is misled by his own metaphor. The possibility of alternative historical accounts encourages White (and perhaps his readers) to conceive of these as subjective and wishful constructions upon a reality which, at best, displays only temporal order rather than intelligible connections of various kinds of causality. The underlying model of time used by White is therefore Kantian: the past is a mere series of disconnected moments of which any historical synthesis is a subjective, ideal construction. As I have shown, however, it is exactly this model of time which Gray's writing subverts and satirises. The story of *1982 Janine* is one in which the protagonist recovers from an inability to narrate the past, an incapacity which – as the text itself shows – has strong connections with the temporal phenomenalism of such modernist devices as "involuntary memory". When Jock resolves to tell his "story in the difficult oldfashioned way, placing events in the order they befell" (Gray 1985a: 192), Gray's writing sets itself against the model of time and history expounded by White. A similar point can be made about *Lanark*, when Lanark disciplines himself in order to overcome the easy attractions of a life without history: "The past seemed a muddle of memories without sequence, like a confused pile of old photographs. To sort them out he tried recalling his life from the start" (Gray 1987: 517).

The clear distinction between White's view of history, and the view of temporality in Gray's fiction, suggests that perhaps the strand of postmodern thought closest to Gray is the Marxist analysis of Fredric Jameson. According to Jameson, "postmodernism" is the cultural expression of "late capitalism", a period where there arises an endemic loss of temporality. This loss of historical experience, claims Jameson, is analogous to a schizophrenic's (supposed) inability to synthesise words into semantically and syntactically coherent utterances:

If we are unable to unify the past, present, and future of the sentence, then we are similarly unable to unify the past, present, and future of our own biographical experience or psychic life. With the breakdown of the signifying chain, therefore, the schizophrenic is reduced to an experience of pure material signifiers, or, in other words, a series of pure and unrelated presents in time. (Jameson 1991: 27)

For Jameson, the personality demanded by "late capitalism" is therefore like a Kantian subject deprived of the faculty of imagination:

If, indeed, the subject has lost its capacity actively to extend its pro-tensions and re-tensions across the temporal manifold and to organize its past and future into coherent experience, it becomes difficult enough to see how the cultural productions of such a subject could result in anything but "heaps of fragments" and in a practice of the randomly heterogeneous and fragmentary and the aleatory. (Jameson 1991: 25)

Indeed, Kate Dryhope – in all probability acting as Gray's mouthpiece – provides the following, and similar, diagnosis of postmodernism in *A History Maker*:

> Postmodernism happened when landlords, businessmen, brokers and bankers who owned the rest of the world had used new technologies to destroy the power of labour unions. Like owners of earlier empires they felt that history had ended because they and their sort could now dominate the world for ever. This indifference to most people's wellbeing and taste appeared in the fashionable art of the wealthy. Critics called their period *postmodern* to separate it from the modern world begun by the Renaissance when most creative thinkers believed they could improve their community. Postmodernists had no interest in the future, which they expected to be an amusing rearrangement of things they already knew. (Gray 1995: 202–3)

But there are differences between Gray's work and Jameson's analysis – and it would be unjust to ignore or trivialise them, or to treat Jameson's ideas as necessarily superior. Gray tends to present "insane" experience as potentially meaningful, or as a voyage of disintegration and re-integration. This puts him at odds with Jameson, who assents to some rather traditional ideas about the unintelligibility of psychotic experience. The latter's argument that a loss of historical temporality is analogous to psychosis derives from Lacan, who asserts that schizophrenia is based upon the inability to relate "signifiers" to other "signifiers". Without such a process of referring words to other words (which generates a so-called "meaning effect"), then schizophrenia is supposed to occur: "when the links of the signifying chain snap", writes Jameson, "then we have schizophrenia in the form of a rubble of distinct and unrelated signifiers" (Jameson 1991: 27). Yet, it was precisely this idea that is criticised by the psychiatric tradition which influences Gray. Laing, for example, sees in the "rubble" of psychotic utterances (or the "word salad", to use the more traditional term), existentially meaningful expressions which could be understood by a suitably empathetic interpreter.

A further difference between Gray and Jameson occurs in their varying ideas on the source of the postmodern loss of temporality. Jameson relates postmodern temporality to the marketing of culture. He argues that the past cannot be represented through commodified cultural forms, and takes as a paradigm the "nostalgia film", a genre of pastiche which

> does not reinvent a picture of the past in its lived totality; rather, by reinventing the feel and shape of characteristic art objects of an older period [...] it seeks to reawaken a sense of the past associated with those objects. (Jameson 1998: 8)

Confronted with this widespread obliteration of true historical consciousness, the postmodern artist, Jameson argues, has little choice but to speak a barbaric "postmodernist 'nostalgia' art language" which is incompatible with "genuine historicity" (Jameson 1991: 19). Gray, on the other hand, often connects a loss of historical thinking with high culture rather than mass culture. Jock McLeish's allusion to Proust, for example, clearly associates the abandonment of historical thought with high-cultural ideas such as the psychology of involuntary memory (and, through that, the influential ideas of philosophers such as Schopenhauer and Kant). There is in both Jameson and Gray a commitment to historical agency – but Gray's work is closer in spirit to existentialism than Marxism, and far more critical of the temporality of high-cultural narrative. There is no easy *rapprochement* between Gray's Laing-influenced writing and Jameson's critical theory.

There are obstacles, then, to either a "textualist" or a Marxist postmodern reading of Gray's work. These problems are less severe for a Jamesonian reading, but nonetheless they impede any straightforward assimilation of Gray's work to "postmodern" theories.

How "Gray" is postmodernism?

An interesting possibility presents itself at this point. If Gray, the seeming postmodernist, is really moved by existential issues of freedom, temporality and historical agency, might other so-called postmodernists offer similar possibilities for revised readings? A detailed consideration of this issue is beyond the scope of the present work. A brief examination of one canonical "post-modernist" can, though, elaborate on the idea that certain "postmodern" authors may have been misunderstood in ways that obscure their parallels with Gray.

In Kurt Vonnegut's novel *Slaughterhouse-Five* (1969), the protagonist Billy Pilgrim (who is loosely based on Vonnegut himself, a survivor of the firestorm at Dresden while an Allied POW), is beset by what may be a delusion, or what may be a marvellous first for humanity. According to Billy, he is one night abducted from his post-war suburban home by aliens from the planet Tralfamadore, who then put him on exhibition in an interstellar zoo. Billy claims that, having returned to Earth (instantaneously, it would seem to Earthlings), he must now dedicate himself to spreading the word of the Tralfamadorians, who have revealed to him the underlying nature of reality:

> All moments, past, present, and future, always have existed, always will exist. The Tralfamadorians can look at all the different moments just the way we can look at a stretch of the Rocky Mountains, for instance. They can see how permanent all the moments are, and they can look at any moment that interests them. It is just an illusion we have here on Earth that one moment follows another one, like beads on a string, and that once a moment is gone it is gone forever. (Vonnegut 1991: 19–20)

Vonengut's narrative then seems to borrow this Tralfamadorian worldview, for Billy accordingly becomes unstuck in time as his narrative leapfrogs around the various moments which comprise his life.

For the postmodern-minded critics of Vonnegut, the Tralfamadorians are to be taken seriously. Jerome Klinkowitz, for example, sees the Tralfamadorians' revelation as a postmodern offer of the only freedom possible in this world. The freedom, that is, to re-arrange not reality, but our representations of it:

> *Slaughterhouse-Five*, with its conscientious attention to the writer's art of rearranging the elements of his story until they make sense to him, gives the readers the chance to experience the world in fresh new ways, and not be prisoners of any one culture's typical forms of description. It may be, philosophers of Vonnegut's age have argued, that not realizing how arbitrary any one formal description is makes people prisoners of a fate that need not be endured. (Klinkowitz 1990: 105–6)

At the heart of Klinkowitz's interpretation is a Kantian (or Tralfamadorian) account of temporality:

> The action depicted within those pages is not determinedly chronological; instead, the author has selected and ordered those pieces of action for an effect other than the inexorable march of history [...]. If history is like a movie, a series of events experienced as a continuous presence but adding up to a final product, why can it not be run backwards rather than always experienced the same way? (Klinkowitz 1990: 104)

For Klinkowitz, time can essentially be compared to cinematography. Past, present, and future are composed of moments which are, like the frames of a movie, normally run together to give a chronological flow of time. With this conceptualisation of time comes the corollary that it must be possible, in principle, to re-arrange these snapshots into a more pleasing and edifying order. This, indeed, is what the aliens suggest to Billy: "the Tralfamadorians would advise

Billy to concentrate on the happy moments of his life, and to ignore the unhappy ones – to stare only at pretty things as eternity failed to go by" (Vonnegut 1991: 142). The best model for this selectivity is Tralfamadorian literature:

> each clump of symbols is a brief, urgent message – describing a situation, a scene. [...] There isn't any particular relationship between all the messages, except that the author has chosen them carefully, so that, when seen all at once, they produce an image of life that is beautiful and surprising and deep. There is no beginning, no middle, no end, no suspense, no moral, no causes, no effects. (Vonnegut 1991: 64)

The self-reflexive elements of Vonnegut's novel, however, undo this facile interpretation. Certainly, there is in his narrative a scepticism towards a certain kind of historical form. Historical explanation, though, is not in itself Vonnegut's target. He is revolted solely by the possibility of reading war as an element in a *providential* history. The underlying narrative of *Slaughterhouse-Five* could easily turn into the story of biographical fulfilment implied by the blurb in the Vintage paperback edition:

> Kurt Vonnegut was born in Indianapolis in 1922 and studied biochemistry at Cornell University. During the Second World War he served in Europe and, as a prisoner of war in Germany, witnessed the destruction of Dresden by Allied bombers, an experience which later inspired this classic novel. (Vonnegut 1991: i)

The possibility of providentially reading his experience in Dresden therefore haunts Vonnegut:

> The Dresden atrocity, tremendously expensive and meticulously planned, was so meaningless, finally, that only one person on the entire planet got any benefit from it. I am that person. I wrote this book, which earned lots of money for me and made my reputation, such as it is. (cited in Klinkowitz 1990: 43)

In the complacent teleological interpretation to which Vonnegut satirically alludes, his personal fulfilment as a writer would, by an enormous moral inversion, bloom in the fertile ash of Dresden. (This possible self-understanding is by no means unlikely: Norman Mailer, for example, found in his wartime experience the materials for a book he had already started *before* he had enlisted – as if the Second World War had happened so that he could then write *The Naked and the Dead* (see Merrill 1978: 26).)

Vonnegut therefore does not turn against historical narrative as a whole. As his novel makes clear, the temporal anarchy of Billy's alien abductors has its own, and rather suspect, earthly parallels. The work of Louis-Ferdinand Céline is amongst Vonnegut's reading material on his post-war return to Dresden: "My other book was Erika Ostrovsky's *Céline and His Vision*. Céline was a brave French soldier in the First World War – until his skull was cracked" (Vonnegut 1991: 15). After this injury, Céline is, like Billy Pilgrim, offended by the seeming reality of generation and destruction:

> Time obsessed him. Miss Ostrovsky reminded me of the amazing scene in *Death on the Installment Plan* where Céline wants to stop the bustling of a street crowd. He screams on paper, *Make them stop ... don't let them move anymore at all ... There, make them freeze ... once and for all! ... So that they won't disappear anymore!* (Vonnegut 1991: 15–16)

Such an ability to freeze time is exactly what the Tralfamadorians grant to Billy: "The most important thing I learned on Tralfamadore was that when a person dies he only *appears* to die. He is still very much alive in the past, so it is very silly for people to cry at his funeral" (Vonnegut 1991: 19).

The Céline connection raises a few sinister associations. Like Graves, Pound, Yeats, and Eliot, he was a modernist who was drawn to extreme right-wing views. His pamphlet *Bagatelles pour un massacre* (1937) is, as Patrick McCarthy records, "overwhelmingly anti-semitic" (McCarthy 1975: 168). Céline "explains how the Russian revolution was financed by American-Jewish bankers" (McCarthy 1975: 152) and, in the face of the growing Nazi menace, fatalistically advocates "pacifism at any price" – including the occupation of France (McCarthy 1975: 149). Billy Pilgrim also preaches quietism and submission. He attempts, for example, to enlighten a boy whose father has been killed in Vietnam: "Billy [...] assured the fatherless boy that his father was very much alive still in moments the boy would see again and again" (Vonnegut 1991: 97–98). Ultimately, the Tralfamadorian gospel is one of fatalism: whether it be to the Vietnam war, the firebombing of Dresden, or even – one assumes – the rise of Nazism, the attitude is one of *Que será, será*. Billy's alien friends therefore simply dismiss free will as a phenomenal illusion: "If I hadn't spent so much time studying Earthlings" says one Tralfamadorian, "I wouldn't have any idea what was meant by 'free will'" (Vonnegut 1991: 62). This fatalism reduces to an obviously absurd conclusion when Billy finds out that the universe will accidentally be destroyed by the Tralfamadorians during a test-flight:

"If you know this," said Billy, "isn't there some way you can prevent it? Can't you keep the pilot from *pressing* the button?"

"He has *always* pressed it, and he always *will*. We *always* let him and we always *will* let him. The moment is *structured* that way." (Vonnegut 1991: 84)

With this comes the corollary that, as Billy says, "the idea of preventing war on Earth is stupid, too" (Vonnegut 1991: 84). As Leonard Mustazza notes, because of the Tralfamadorian attitude to time, Billy acquires "a deterministic existence in which nothing needs to be explained or rectified since free will can do nothing to change conditions" (Mustazza 1990: 114).

The phenomenalist premise that the future is foreknowable leads, then, to an abolition of contingency and to a consequent negation of moral responsibility. Vonnegut therefore makes modernist narrative techniques strange and unfamiliar to the reader so that she can then conceptualise them, and so articulate some of the consequences which follow upon the modernist obsession with a temporally fragmented inner-life. This is why the Tralfamadorians are used to describe temporal phenomenalism: what better way is there to defamiliarise modernist narratology than to espouse it through the mouth of an alien? In *Slaughterhouse-Five*, we follow a narrative which, when set against its subject matter, leads us to perceive the complicity between its modernist form and the amnesiac complacency of America during the post-war period. As Merrill and Scholl conclude,

The object of satiric attack turns out to be a complacent response to the horrors of the age. The horror of Dresden is not just that it *could* happen here, in an enlightened twentieth-century. The real horror is that events such as Dresden continue to occur and no one seems appalled. (Merrill and Scholl 1990: 149)

Like Gray, Vonnegut uses metafictional strategies and narratological innovations not in the service of some postmodern world-construction or destabilisation of "Truth" and "History", but rather to subvert the quietism that may be encoded in the act of reading (particularly in the act of reading modernist literature). The comparison with Gray extends further: for amongst Vonnegut's satiric targets are the modernists whose retreat into subjectivity licensed a submission to right-wing authoritarian regimes – Céline and Graves, after all, are not so politically distant.

Is Gray post-nationalist?

Gray is not postmodern in any accepted sense; but may he be recogisably "postnational"? Many recent theorists and critics have come to regard our own age as one in which traditional certainties about nationality (and nationalism) are in decline. Nations no longer seem the dominant ordering principle of society in an era of global economy, multicultural territories, and sub- and supra-national political structures. Postnational theory often confronts literature – especially in Scotland – when it criticises literary projections of a homogeneous national culture. Eleanor Bell's work, for example, thoroughly criticises the tendency (perhaps more apparent in criticism than literature) to posit some kind of typical Scottishness. The problem, she argues, is that, for most of the twentieth century, Scottish literature and criticism were a vehicle for thwarted political ambitions. In order to make Scottish culture more politically significant, it became a useful strategy to pretend that there was a common Scottish culture (even if it was pathological and damaged) upon which Scottishness was based.

In *Questioning Scotland* (2004), Bell illustrates some of the problems of such a reductive self-definition. She points out how the critic Alan Bold complacently refers in an article to the "typical Scot" – someone who is male, miserable, envious of success, and possessed of a sense of inferiority to the English. As Bell points out:

> The notion of the average Scot as inferior has also been a recurrent trope in Scottish cultural criticism, yet the repetition of such recurrent themes does not make them unproblematic, or somehow an epitome of the Scottish psyche. (Bell 2004b: 36)

Scottish cultural criticism has, through such repetition, become a minefield of "questionable generalisation", "fixed characteristics" and "definitive statements" (Bell 2004b: 49). The fundamental problem for Bell is the one that I mentioned in my introduction: that of cultural essentialism. One of her key metaphors is of "stereotyping" – the idea that Scottish culture is like a cast printing plate (rather than a matrix of movable type) which stamps out endless copies of the same unrevisable edition of *The National Psyche*. There surely cannot be, she argues, some essence to being a Scot, some total (necessary) and exclusive (sufficient) criteria which might – for example – bolster the legitimacy of Scottish political ambitions.

Regardless of whether or not Bell accurately represents the work of Tom Nairn, Cairns Craig, and others, it is necessary to ask – in the present context – whether my study of Gray's work falls into the trap of stereotyping, and, indeed, whether Gray's work (which is clearly politically nationalist) itself has truck with notions of essential Scottishness.

I was concerned in my introduction to argue that my own critical approach – which frequently has recourse to the history of ideas in Scotland – should not be regarded as essentialist. My approach seemed to me necessary because of a neglect of Scottish ideas in criticism of Scottish literature; this ignorance, I argued, could be traced to a sizeable dose of cultural inferiorism. Of course, I do not regard the "Scottish cringe" as necessary and sufficient to some supposed Scottish identity. Indeed, how could I? – for though I would identify myself as Scottish, I do not regard Scottish culture as trivial.

I therefore argued that reading Scottish literature in relation to Scottish ideas is a necessary response to an earlier cultural essentialism which argued for the essentially emotive nature of the Scottish psyche. A similar argument is advanced by Richard Kearney, the doyen of postnational theorising of Irish culture. He refers to "the two ideological prejudices most responsible for the eclipse of Irish minds in [Irish] cultural history": the "colonial" and the "cultural nationalist" (Kearney 1997: 171). "The first takes the form of the old imperialist view that if someone can think s/he cannot be Irish"; and the second arises in the reaction against colonialism – "While Irish mythology was being proudly restored by our Cultural Revival at the turn of the century (and rightly so), Irish science and philosophy were unconscionably ignored" (Kearney 1997: 172). The parallels in Scottish culture might be the dismissal of Scots as backward by English culture (identified by Craig Beveridge and Ronald Turnbull), and a modernist obsession with a supposed Scots physicality in the Scottish Renaissance.

What of Gray's work, though? Do his creative and political writings – which carry a clear nationalist manifesto – advance the idea of an essential Scottishness?

Gray is certainly opposed to the cultural essentialism of the British Empire. In *1982 Janine* there occurs a scene – typical of post-war Scottish literature – in which a Scottish schoolmaster tries to impose linguistic homogeneity upon his society. Hislop punishes a boy for using the word "jaggy" as an antonym to "blunt", and tells him: "your employment of local slang is either a conscious or unconscious effort to destroy communication between the provinces of a once mighty empire. Are you a linguistic saboteur or are you an idiot?"

(Gray 1985a: 84). Indeed, Jock's greatest act of childhood courage – which he recalls as he recovers from his schizoid condition – is to intervene when Hislop finally breaks down and endlessly punishes a boy who speaks with a lisp.

Of course, Gray could conceivably anticipate a fragmentation of the British state into culturally homogeneous pieces – perhaps as Scottish, Welsh, Irish, and English mini-empires. For a certain kind of theory of nationalism, this expectation would be almost inevitable. Ernst Gellner, for example, argues that nationalism is the cultural reflex of modernisation. The production and reception of modern context-free communications (instructions, order, designs, plans, and so on) requires a common culture, and particularly a common language, in order to maximise the hermeneutic efficiency of a society (see Gellner 1997). Even analyses which – unlike Gellner's – do more justice to the existential meaning of nationalism, might seem to posit an almost inevitable connection between nationalism and a (potentially sinister) cultural unity. Anthony D. Smith provides an understanding of nationalism which emphasises the religious meaning of the phenomenon. In the USA, for example, "saluting the flag, celebrating public holidays, the cult of the Constitution, and the founding fathers, commemorations of the glorious war dead, and so on" form what he calls a "secular religion" (Smith, Anthony D. 2001: 42). Such observances not only legitimate a common culture useful for modern society, they

> supplement and sometimes supplant traditional religious faith in an after-life, which they transfer to an earthly plane, with a promise of collective immortality carried in and through the yet unborn generations of the nation. (Smith, Anthony D. 2001: 35)

Smith's analysis presents some concepts which resonate with the reading of Gray's work which I have presented. He argues that "four basic categories of the nation – community, territory, history and destiny" form "what one might term the 'sacred properties' of the nation or, more accurately, the basic properties of the nation conceived as a sacred communion of its members" (Smith, Anthony D. 2001: 144). The sacred communion of a nation does not typically involve a symbolic meal like Catholic communion (though there are occasional instances of this, such as the simultaneous national communion of Thanksgiving in the USA). The communion of citizen with nation occurs more often in the various rituals by which the members of a national congregation can participate in the destiny of one nation elected under God:

> The privilege of [national] election is afforded only to those who are sanctified, whose life-style is an expression of sacred values. The benefits of election are reserved for those who fulfil the required observances. (Smith, Anthony D. 1999: 130)

The relevance of Smith's concepts to my reading of Gray is clear enough. For Smith, nationalism may provide a "sacred communion" – a spiritual communion much like that which I identified, for example, in the schizoid relation of Thaw to his White Goddess, Hjordis to the imaginary Harry, or – outside of Gray's work – in the writings of George Friel and Nan Shepherd. If Gray's work is to be at all consistent, then whatever brand of nationalism he espouses must refuse the idea that a nation is a sacred communion of members who participate in a uniquely fated national destiny. Such sacred nationalism would merely be the large-scale political parallel to the spiritual communion and temporal phenomenalism that is so often satirised and subverted in his writings.

Fortunately, both for the consistency of my reading, and for the value of Gray's nationalism, the religious function of nationalism seems to be criticised, rather than upheld, in his work. In *The Fall of Kelvin Walker*, Kelvin is led back to Scotland by his father, who has recently humiliated him on national television (reducing him, as we have seen, to a state of Laingean petrification). As Kelvin's Calvinist beliefs in predestination re-emerge in all their glory, his father offers him a future based on a myth of sacred national communion: "[We Scots are] a neglected province. A despised province. But four hundred years back we conceived ourselves to be a Chosen People. We had a leader then" (Gray 1986: 137). Kelvin is unable to refuse this invitation to be a new John Knox for Scotland, and so returns to Scotland, where he rises to political power, and eventually becomes "293rd Moderator of the General Assembly of the United Seceders Free Presbyterian Church of Scotland" (Gray 1986: 141). He becomes an utterly predictable guardian of traditional morality, and, in fact, stymies any efforts to devolve Scotland – it seems that only by remaining "neglected" and "despised" may Scots continue to perform their national observances. As the narrator remarks, the English – though perhaps equally caught up in myths of national identity – do not find that misery is a patriotic duty. Kelvin's erstwhile London friends, Jake and Jill, go onto have a couple of children.

The narrator tells us: "These children are often happy. / It is easier for them. / They are English" (Gray 1986: 141).

Gray's destruction of myths of national (or societal) election is also apparent in the two short stories "The Start of the Axletree" and "The End of the Axletree" (1979). The Axletree is a gigantic conical tower-cum-pyramid begun by the emperor of the "great wheel", a continent-wide civilisation which binds together some forty-three nations. In an effort to maintain the unity of his society (which seems to be an allegory of the Roman Empire), the emperor consults with a sage, and returns with an inspired plan to construct a building which links earth to sky. This absurd scheme, which acts as a rationale for the empire's economic rapacity, is immediately given a religious gloss by the high priest, who declares,

> all dreams are sacred, and the dreams of a ruler are most sacred of all. Perhaps the heavenly gods are growing lonely. Perhaps mankind is becoming fit to join them. Let us tell the world this dream. You may be the prophet who will lead us all to the golden garden in the sky. (Gray 1984c: 81–82)

Gray's allegory then traces the myth of the axletree through various parallels for the development of European society. The axletree changes from an allegorised Catholic Church – "a shining structure with a single summit revered by the whole continent" (Gray 1984c: 260) – into a divided enterprise when a "protesting agent" (Gray 1984c: 240) quarrels with the "foreman" (Gray 1984c: 239). In the ensuing conflict between forces of foreman and agent (between Catholic and Protestant Christianity),

> leaders on both sides started squabbling – each was a king on his own lands and disliked sharing his gains with the rest. So by mutual agreement, by force or by fraud the great work was split into as many sections as the surrounding nations. (Gray 1984c: 243)

All these societies then strive to build higher, and to achieve the sacred communion that would demonstrate their unique selection by the deity. In the ensuing competition between these sacred nations, there arises an age like that of European imperialism, in which "remote people" are forced to supply materials for "God's great unfinished house in the middle of the world" (Gray 1984c: 242). After the wars which follow this period, the "national companies" (Gray 1984c: 242) form into two groups, the "construction companies" (capitalist societies) and the "co-operatives" (communist societies) which then continue the competition to build the axletree (Gray 1984c:

244). Gray's story concludes when one of the companies eventually reaches, and then breaches, the sky, and the Axletree is destroyed in a flood of water (a metaphor for nuclear holocaust).

As this allegory makes clear, Gray is keenly aware of the myths of national election which can turn a nation into a form of sacred, rather than political, communion. Like the schizoid communion with an imaginary other, the supposed contact between nation and deity (manifest in a national fatalism) is a destructive withdrawal from true communion with others, and submission to a predetermined temporality. The apocalypse at the end of the Axletree stories is the global analogue to the personal destruction which devours Thaw (and which threatens Jock McLeish and many other of Gray's characters).

The positive content of Gray's political nationalism is set out in the revised version of *Why Scots Should Rule Scotland*. The start of this 1987 pamphlet, however, may seem unpromising, for Gray claims that his argument "is not based on differences of race, religion, or language, but geology" (Gray 1984c: 2). This seems to invite either some peculiar geographical-political determinism, or, perhaps, a mystical identification between Scots and the land. But as the text's references to "the lie of the land" suggest (Gray 1984c: 4), the use of geology is a cover, "a lie", for a political metaphor. According to Gray, "Firths, sea lochs, chains of high moorlands and mountains made north Britain like a cluster of big islands jammed together in the east and coming apart in the west" (Gray 1984c: 2–3). Gray deftly employs a non-essentialist symbolism: what is central to Scotland is what is "marginal" – "Scotland is a cluster of islands, most of them not separated by water" (Gray 1984c: 110). By making Scotland "essentially" a group of islands, Gray creates an anti-essentialist vision of Scotland as a mosaic of communities.

Furthermore, Gray's nationalism is "civic" rather than "ethnic". It is closer to the French model whereby, as McCrone reminds us, "whatever one's ethnic or geographical origins, all residents on French soil could in principle be citizens of the French state" (McCrone 1998: 9), unlike the German ethnic model (which still stands today) in which "citizenship was formed on the basis of a community of descent", so that "a child received German citizenship if the parent had it" (McCrone 1998: 9). In Gray's civic nationalism the term "Scots" applies not to the possessors of a common culture, nor to members of an ethnic descent group, but to "everyone in Scotland who is able to vote" (Gray 1984c: 1). Gray therefore excludes ethnic Scots "who live and vote abroad", but includes "many who feel thoroughly English", as well as "second or third generation half-breeds" (Gray 1984c: 1): the "English, Irish, Chinese, Indian, Polish, Italian and Russian Jewish" are the non-geographical "islanders" who comprise Gray's diverse Scots. Indeed, this "island" model of the nation expands into Gray's vision of an international community. In the 1950s, he hoped that the world would become a conglomerate of small, more-or-less socialist countries, analogous to the well-ordered society found in the housing estate of Riddrie in which he was brought up: "I expected the world to become a mosaic of Riddries, each with a strong local favour of course" (Gray 1984c: 96–97).

Gray's memories of Riddrie contain further clarification of his politics. Not only is his nationalism non-ethnic, it also offers an alternative to the transcendental sacred communion satirised in the Axletree stories:

> There was also a Protestant and a Catholic church, but my parents had not forced the burden of an immortal soul upon me, so to me the spiritual and mental power-house of Riddrie and also (when I was old enough to get political convictions) the pinnacle of socialist civilization was the public library. (Gray 1984c: 96)

At the centre of Gray's particular island is a non-sectarian secular "church" "that anybody could enter" in order to "browse through [a] warm quiet treasury of alternative worlds" (Gray 1984c: 96). Instead of the single transcendental alternative world offered by a nation confident of its sacred destiny, there is instead a cosmopolitan plurality of alternative earthly worlds offered by such writers as Blake, Heine, Hogg, Sartre, and Thurber.

It should by now be clear that Gray's nationalism is very far from being ethnic, essentialist, quasi-religious or introverted. In fact, given Gray's Scottish context, it would be very difficult for his nationalism to be otherwise. As David McCrone observes, Scottish nationalism is almost inevitably civic: "Scottishness is based on living in a common territory despite clear and abiding social, religious and geographical differences" (McCrone 1998: 22). This puts Gray's nationalism (like Scottish nationalism as whole) amongst the political movements which McCrone identifies as "neo-nationalisms" (McCrone 1998: 125–48). Whether or not such "neo-nationalist" status qualifies Gray as "postnationalist" is a matter of semantics best left to students of the latter term. Let it be noted though, that the neo-nationalist movements in Scotland, Quebec and Catalunya are not the monstrous ethnic nationalisms of early twentieth-century imperial nations. Instead they are civic nationalisms, which are hard-headed, economically aware, and which co-exist with multiple identities to supra-national structures (such as the European Union) and sub-national collectivities.

Conclusion

Gray's work is not postmodern in a recognised sense – unless we redefine postmodernism so that the metafiction of Gray and Vonnegut becomes central. Barring this unlikely development, Gray must be understood as something else – as a writer whose self-reflexive and playful fictions are the formal correlate of a content that has little to do with postmodern or post-structural ideas. The affinities of his work with the ideas of R.D. Laing and Jean-Paul Sartre mean that Gray is closest in spirit to existentialism, albeit an existentialism with a particularly strong insistence on the reality and value of communion between persons, and a corresponding scepticism towards the cultic and mythic tendencies of modernist literature.

But though Gray is not postmodern, he is "post-" ethnic and cultural nationalism. Many of his texts critique a schizoid relation with imaginary others – be this Thaw with the moon goddess, Jock McLeish with his imaginary lovers, or even the make-believe relationship between the reader and the supratemporal narrator. Since the nation too may provide a kind of spiritual, transcendent communion, Gray's work also undoes myths of national destiny and the election of an exclusive "chosen people". This opposition to essentialist views of the nation arises from the particular logic of his writings, however, rather than from his immersion in any supposed universal "postmodern predicament".

I have argued for a particular interpretation of Gray's writing; but, in so doing, I have also tried to make a methodological point. It is very easy for contemporary critical approaches of a broadly postmodern kind to seize the ethical high ground. By endless repetition of words such as "diversity", "de-centring" and "polyphony", and by a proclaimed commitment to "feminising the word", or allowing the "subaltern" to speak, such theories achieve an almost hypnotic persuasiveness: to allow marginalised voices to be heard, it seems obvious that we must adopt these methods.

However, by doing something rather more conventional – by reading Gray in his literary and intellectual context – I have actually detected the voice that postmodernist readings cannot hear. Too often, what is distinctive and interesting in Gray is lost in a blizzard of well-intentioned postmodern readings that consider his work in abstraction. In one recent postmodern reading of Gray's *Poor Things*, for example, the US author's acquaintance with Scottish ideas is minimal: Gray's text is passed to him by a friend who finds it in a pile of remaindered books (see Kaczvinsky 2001). This is how Gray's work frequently appears in the international market of ideas – as a bargain-basement illustration of what everyone already "knows" about "postmodern" literature. Instead of protecting smaller cultures, such analyses are – to be blunt – a form of cultural imperialism emanating (primarily) from the academic institutions of the USA. I hope that this book will stop that unfortunate process by redirecting scholarly attention to the cosmopolitan depth and richness of twentieth-century Scottish culture.

Bibliography

Ackerman, Robert. 1987. *J.G. Frazer: His Life and Work*. Cambridge: Cambridge University Press.
Adorno, Theodor W. and Max Horkheimer. 1979. *Dialectic of Enlightenment* (tr. Cumming, John). London: Verso.
Augustine. 1981. *Concerning the City of God against the Pagans* (tr. Bettenson, Henry). Harmondsworth: Penguin.
Axelrod, Mark. 1995. "An Epistolary Interview, Mostly with Alasdair Gray" in *Review of Contemporary Fiction* 15.2: 106–15.
Banks, Iain. 1988. *Espedair Street*. London: Abacus.
Bell, Eleanor. 2004a. "Postmodernism, Nationalism, and the Question of Tradition" in Bell, Eleanor and Gavin Miller (eds) *Scotland in Theory: Reflections on Literature and Culture*. Amsterdam and New York: Rodopi. 83–95.
—. 2004b. *Questioning Scotland: Literature, Nationalism, Postmodernism*. Basingstoke: Palgrave Macmillan.
Bernstein, Stephen. 1999. *Alasdair Gray*. Lewisburg: Bucknell University Press.
The Bible. 1997. Oxford: Oxford University Press.
Boyd, S.J. 1991. "Black Arts: *1982 Janine* and *Something Leather*" in Crawford, Robert and Thom Nairn (eds) *The Arts of Alasdair Gray*. Edinburgh: Edinburgh University Press. 108–23.
Brecht, Berthold. 1974. "Short Description of a New Technique of Acting which Produces an Alienation Effect" in *Brecht on Theatre: The Development of an Aesthetic*. London: Methuen: 136–47.
Bucknall, Barbara. 1969. *The Religion of Art in Proust*. Urbana: University of Illinois Press.
Burston, Daniel. 1996. *The Wing of Madness: The Life and Work of R.D. Laing*. Cambridge, Mass. and London: Harvard University Press.
Cameron, Iain. 1987. *George Friel: an Introduction to his Life and Work*. MLitt thesis (unpub.). Department of English Literature. University of Edinburgh.
Clay, John. 1996. *R.D. Laing: A Divided Self: A Biography*. London: Hodder and Stoughton.
Concise Oxford Dictionary. 1976. Oxford: Oxford University Press.
Craig, Cairns. 1982. *Yeats, Eliot, Pound and the Politics of Poetry: Richest to the Richest*. London and Canberra: Croom Helm.
—. 1991. "Going Down to Hell is Easy" in Crawford, Robert and Thom Nairn (eds) *The Arts of Alasdair Gray*. Edinburgh: Edinburgh University Press. 90–107.
—. 1999. *The Modern Scottish Novel: Narrative and the National Imagination*. Edinburgh: Edinburgh University Press.
—. 2004. "Scotland and Hybridity" in Carruthers, Gerard, David Goldie and Alastair Renfrew (eds) *Beyond Scotland: New Contexts for Twentieth-Century Scottish Literature*. Amsterdam and New York: Rodopi. 227–51.
Day, Douglas. 1963. *Swifter than Reason: The Poetry and Criticism of Robert Graves*. Chapel Hill, N.C.: University of North Carolina.
de Juan, Luis. 2003. *Postmodernist Strategies in Alasdair Gray's Lanark: a Life in 4 Books*. Frankfurt am Main: Peter Lang.
de Wulf, M. c.1907. *Scholasticism Old and New: An Introduction to Scholastic Philosophy Medieval and Modern*. Dublin: Gill.

Fairbairn, W. Ronald D. 1952a. "A Revised Psychopathology of the Psychoses and Neuroses" in *Psychoanalytic Studies of the Personality.* London: Tavistock. 28–58.
—. 1952b. "Schizoid Factors in the Personality" in *Psychoanalytic Studies in the Personality.* London: Tavistock. 3–27.
—. 1994. "Re-evaluating Some Basic Concepts" in Scharff, David E. and Ellinor Fairbairn Birtles (eds) *From Instinct to Self: Selected Papers of W.R.D. Fairbairn Volume 1: Clinical and Theoretical Papers.* London: Jason Aronson. 129–38.
Frazer, J.G. 1987. *The Golden Bough: A Study in Magic and Religion.* Abridged edn. London: Pan Macmillan.
Freud, Sigmund. 1953. *The Interpretation of Dreams (first part)* (tr. Strachey, James and others). London: Hogarth.
Friel, George. 1994. *The Bank of Time.* Edinburgh: Polygon.
—. 1999. *A Glasgow Trilogy: The Boy Who Wanted Peace; Grace and Miss Partridge; Mr Alfred, MA.* Edinburgh: Canongate.
Fuss, Diana. 1990. *Essentially Speaking: Feminism, Nature and Difference.* London: Routledge.
Gardiner, Michael. 2004. *The Cultural Roots of British Devolution.* Edinburgh: Edinburgh University Press.
Gellner, Ernest. 1997. *Nationalism.* London: Weidenfeld & Nicolson.
Genette, Gerard. 1980. *Narrative Discourse: An Essay in Method.* Ithaca, New York: Cornell University.
Graves, Robert. 1952. *The White Goddess: A Grammar of Poetical Myth.* 3rd edn. London: Faber and Faber.
Gray, Alasdair. 1984a. ""Five Letters from an Eastern Empire"" in *Unlikely Stories, Mostly.* London: Penguin.
—. 1984b. "The Great Bear Cult" in *Unlikely Stories, Mostly.* London: Penguin. 44–66.
—. 1984c. "The Start of the Axletree; The End of the Axletree" in *Unlikely Stories, Mostly.* London: Penguin. 67–84, 233–71.
—. 1985a. *1982 Janine.* Harmondsworth, Middlesex: Penguin.
—. 1985b. *Lean Tales.* London: Jonathan Cape.
—. 1986. *The Fall of Kelvin Walker.* Rev. edn. Harmondsworth, Middlesex: Penguin.
—. 1987. *Lanark: A Life in Four Books.* London: Collins.
—. 1990. *Something Leather.* London: Jonathan Cape.
—. 1992. *Poor Things: Episodes from the Early Life of Archibald McCandless M.D. Scottish Public Health Officer.* London: Bloomsbury.
—. 1993. *Ten Tales Tall & True.* New York: Harcourt Brace.
—. 1995. *A History Maker.* London: Penguin.
—. 1997. *Why Scots Should Rule Scotland 1997: A Carnaptious History of Britain from Roman Times Until Now.* Edinburgh: Canongate.
—. 2000. *Sixteen Occasional Poems: 1990–2000.* Glasgow: Morag McAlpine.
Gunn, Neil M. 1937. *Highland River.* Edinburgh: Porpoise.
Habermas, Jürgen. 1987. *The Philosophical Discourse of Modernity: Twelve Lectures* (tr. Lawrence, Frederick). Cambridge: Polity with Basil Blackwell.
Hume, David. 1978. *A Treatise of Human Nature.* 2nd edn. Oxford: Oxford University Press.
Hume, Kathryn. 1984. *Fantasy and Mimesis: Responses to Reality in Western Literature.* New York and London: Methuen.

Jackson, Rosemary. 1981. *Fantasy: The Literature of Subversion*. London and New York: Methuen.
Jameson, Fredric. 1991. *Postmodernism, or, the Cultural Logic of Late Capitalism*. London and New York: Verso.
—. 1998. *The Cultural Turn: Selected Writings on the Postmodern 1983–1998*. London and New York: Verso.
Jenkins, Robin. 2000. *Poor Angus*. Edinburgh: Canongate.
Julius, Anthony. 1995. *T.S. Eliot, Anti-Semitism, and Literary Form*. Cambridge: Cambridge University Press.
Kaczvinsky, Donald P. 2001. "'Making Up for Lost Time': Scotland, Stories, and the Self in Alasdair Gray's *Poor Things*" in *Contemporary Literature* 42.4: 775–99.
Kant, Immanuel. 1929. *Critique of Pure Reason* (tr. Kemp Smith, Norman). London: Macmillan.
Kearney, Richard. 1997. *Postnationalist Ireland: Politics, culture, philosophy*. London and New York: Routledge.
Kennedy, A.L. 1998. "Original Bliss" in *Original Bliss*. London: Vintage. 151–311.
King, Elspeth. 2002. "Art for the Early Days of a Better Nation" in Moores, Phil (ed.) *Alasdair Gray: Critical Appreciations and a Bibliography*. Boston Spa and London: The British Library. 93–121.
Klinkowitz, Jerome. 1990. *Slaughterhouse-Five: Reforming the Novel and the World*. Boston: Twayne.
Laing, R.D. 1965. *The Divided Self: An Existential Study in Sanity and Madness*. Harmondsworth, Middlesex: Pelican.
—. 1967. *The Politics of Experience and the Bird of Paradise*. London: Penguin.
—. 1971. "The Politics of the Family" in *The Politics of the Family and Other Essays*. London: Tavistock. 65–124.
—. 1998. *Wisdom, Madness, and Folly: The Making of a Psychiatrist 1927–57*. Edinburgh: Canongate.
Laing, R.D., H. Phillipson and A.R. Lee. 1966. *Interpersonal Perception: A Theory and a Method of Research*. London and New York: Tavistock and Springer.
Lumsden, Alison. 1993. "Innovation and Reaction in the Fiction of Alasdair Gray" in Stevenson, Randall and Gavin Wallace (eds) *The Scottish Novel since the Seventies: New Visions, Old Dreams*. Edinburgh: Edinburgh University.
Mangan, Gerald. 1990. Review of *Something Leather* in *TLS* (6 July 1990). 731.
Marcus, Steven. 1966. *The Other Victorians: A Study of Sexuality and Pornography in Mid-nineteenth-century England*. London: Weidenfeld and Nicolson.
Massie, Allan. 1981. "Glasgow will never be the same after *Lanark*". *The Scotsman* (28 February 1981). 3.
McCarthy, Patrick. 1975. *Céline*. London: Allen Lane.
McCrone, David. 1998. *The Sociology of Nationalism: Tomorrow's ancestors*. London and New York: Routledge.
McHale, Brian. 1987. *Postmodernist Fiction*. New York: Methuen.
Mendelson, Edward (ed.). 1976. *W.H. Auden: Collected Poems*. London: Faber and Faber.
Merrill, Robert. 1978. *Norman Mailer*. Boston: Twayne.
Merrill, Robert and Peter A. Scholl. 1990. "Vonnegut's *Slaughterhouse-Five*: The Requirements of Chaos" in Merrill, Robert (ed.) *Critical Essays on Kurt Vonnegut* Boston: G.K. Hall. 142–52.

Miller, Gavin. 2004a. "'Persuade without convincing … represent without reasoning': the Inferiorist Mythology of the Scots Language" in Bell, Eleanor and Gavin Miller (eds) *Scotland in Theory: Reflections on Literature and Culture*. Amsterdam and New York: Rodopi. 197–209.
—. 2004b. *R.D. Laing*. Edinburgh: Edinburgh University Press.
Mitchison, Naomi. 1985. *Memoirs of a Spacewoman*. London: The Women's Press.
Mullan, Bob. 1995. *Mad to Be Normal: Conversations with R.D. Laing*. London: Free Association.
— (ed.). 1997. *R.D. Laing: Creative Destroyer*. London: Cassell.
Mustazza, Leonard. 1990. *Forever Pursuing Genesis: The Myth of Eden in the Novels of Kurt Vonnegut*. Lewisburg: Bucknell University Press.
Oxford English Dictionary. 1989. 2nd edn. Oxford: Clarendon. vol 2.
Proust, Marcel. 1922. *Swann's Way: Part One* (tr. Moncrieff, C.K. Scott). London: Chatto & Windus.
Reich, Wilhelm. 1950. *Character Analysis* (tr. Wolfe, Theodore P.). London: Vision and Peter Nevill.
—. 1983. *The Function of the Orgasm: Sex-Economic Problems of Biological Energy* (tr. Carfagno, Vincent R.). London: Souvenir.
Robertson Smith, William. 1878–1889. "Sacrifice" in *Encyclopaedia Britannica* 9th edn. 21: 132–38.
—. 1894. *Lectures on the Religion of the Semites: First Series: The Fundamental Institutions*. London: Adam and Charles Black.
—. 1907. *Kinship and Marriage in Early Arabia*. New edn. London: Adam and Charles Black.
Rycroft, Charles. 1971. *Reich*. London: Fontana and Collins.
Sartre, Jean-Paul. 1948. *Existentialism and Humanism* (tr. Mairet, Philip). London: Methuen.
—. 1950. *What is Literature?* (tr. Frechtman, Bernard). London: Methuen.
—. 1967. *Words* (tr. Clephane, Irene). Harmondsworth, Middlesex: Penguin.
—. 1969. *Being and Nothingness: An Essay on Phenomenological Ontology* (tr. Barnes, Hazel E.). London: Routledge.
Schopenhauer, Arthur. 1974. "Transcendent Speculation on the Apparent Deliberateness in the Fate of the Individual" in *Parerga and Paralipomena: Short Philosophical Essays* (tr. Payne, E.F.J.). 2 vols. Oxford: Clarendon. 199–223.
Scriven, Anne. 2004. "The Muted Scotswoman and Oliphant's *Kirsteen*" in Bell, Eleanor and Gavin Miller (eds) *Scotland in Theory: Reflections on Literature and Culture*. Amsterdam and New York: Rodopi. 167–81.
Shepherd, Nan. 1996. *The Grampian Quartet: The Quarry Wood; The Weatherhouse; A Pass in the Grampians; The Living Mountains*. Edinburgh: Canongate.
Smith, Anthony D. 1999. *Myths and Memories of the Nation*. Oxford: Oxford University Press.
—. 2001. *Nationalism: Theory, Ideology, History*. Cambridge and Oxford: Blackwell.
Smith, G. Gregory. 1919. *Scottish Literature: Character and Influence*. London: Macmillan.
Smith, Martin Seymour. 1982. *Robert Graves: His Life and Work*. London: Hutchinson.
Stenhouse, David. 1996. "A Wholly Healthy Scotland: A Reichian Reading of *1982 Janine*" in *Edinburgh Review* 95: 113–22.

Stevenson, Randall. 1991. "Alasdair Gray and the Postmodern" in Crawford, Robert and Thom Nairn (eds) *The Arts of Alasdair Gray*. Edinburgh: Edinburgh University Press. 48–63.
—. 1992. *Modernist Fiction: An Introduction*. Hemel Hempstead, Hertfordshire: Harvester Wheatsheaf.
Sutherland, John. 1996. Review of *Mavis Belfrage* in *TLS* (17 May 1996). 22.
Suttie, Ian D. 1935. *The Origins of Love and Hate*. London: Kegan Paul.
Tiitinen, Johanna. 1999. "A World at the End of History? *A History Maker* by Alasdair Gray" in Cowan, Edward J. and Douglas Gifford (eds) *The Polar Twins*. Edinburgh: John Donald. 270–83.
Todorov, Tzvetan. 1973. *The Fantastic: A Structural Approach to a Literary Genre* (tr. Howards, Richard). Cleveland and London: Case Western Reserve.
Tolstoy, Leo. 1942. "Second Epilogue" in *War and Peace*. London: MacMillan and Oxford University Press. 1305–44.
van Gennep, Arnold. 1960. *The Rites of Passage* (tr. Vizedom, Monika B. and Gabrielle L. Caffee). London: Routledge and Kegan Paul.
Vickery, John B. 1973. *The Literary Impact of The Golden Bough*. Princeton: Princeton University Press.
Vonnegut, Kurt. 1991. *Slaughterhouse-Five or The Children's Crusade: A Duty-Dance with Death*. London: Vintage.
White, Hayden. 1987. *The Content of the Form: Narrative Discourse and Historical Representation*. Baltimore and London: John Hopkins University Press.
Whyte, Christopher. 2004. "Queer Readings, Gay Texts: From *Redgauntlet* to *The Prime of Miss Jean Brodie*" in Bell, Eleanor and Gavin Miller (eds) *Scotland in Theory: Reflections on Literature and Culture*. Amsterdam and New York: Rodopi. 147–65.
Young, Elizabeth. 1992. Review of *Poor Things* in *The Guardian* (3 September 1992). 23.

Index

NUMERICS

1982 Janine (Gray novel)
  cultural essentialism 126
  depersonalisation 65–66
  sexual fantasies 79–80
  sexual repression 55–56
  mental breakdown 73
  Proust, intertextual with 101, 104–106
  Scottish masculinity 21–23

A

Adorno, Theodor 32–34
Auden, W.H. *See* primitivism
St Augustine 95
Axelrod, Mark 55

B

Banks, Iain (M.) 44
Bell, Eleanor 12, 125
Bernstein, Stephen 79, 83, 115
Boyd, S.J. 76
Brecht, Berthold 108
Bucknall, Barbara 103
Burston, Daniel 74, 77

C

Camus, Albert 88
Celine, Louis-Ferdinand 123
Clay, John 57
commensal. *See* communion
communion 16–20
  commensal 18, 37, 40
  companion 16
  corporation 16
  Frazer, J.G. 48
  Holy Communion 16, 20
  kinship 18, 48
  Laing, R.D. 61
  Macmurray, John 19
  morning draught, ritual of 18, 22
  national religion 18, 127
  Proust, Marcel 101
  recognition 17, 66, 90
  sacrifice 18
  Sartrean "shame" as 89
  Scottish culture, importance to 19–20
  Scottish literature, motif in 44–52
  Smith, William Robertson 18, 48
  spiritual/transcendental 23–24, 37–49, 45–52, 92
  reading as 90–93, 100, 110
  van Gennep, Arnold 48
companion. *See* communion
corporation. *See* communion
Craig, Cairns 15, 19, 29, 72, 78–79, 95

D

Day, Douglas 31
de Juan, Luis 87

E

Eliot, T.S. *See* primitivism
essentialism. *See* Scottish literary criticism
existentialism. *See* Sartre, Jean-Paul; Camus, Albert

F

"Five Letters from an Eastern Empire" (Gray short story) 97
The Fall of Kelvin Walker (Gray novella) 63, 91, 93, 128
fantasy. *See also* psychoanalysis
  literary genre 72–73, 78–85
  literary impulse 67
Frazer, J.G. *See* primitivism, communion
Freud, Sigmund. *See* psychoanalysis
Friel, George 47–50, 96
Fuss, Diana 13

G

Gardiner, Michael 19
Gellner, Ernst 127
Genette, Gerard 108, 111
Gibbon, Lewis Grassic Gibbon 19
Graves, Robert. *See* primitivism
Gray, Alasdair
  Britain post-Thatcher 80
  childhood and schooling 9–10
  critical reception 10

existentialism, influence of 88
Graves, Robert, enjoyment of 31
historical conquest, views on 96
homogeneity of work 12
Laing, R.D., influence of 57
literary career 10–12
literary works. *See* individual entries
postmodernism, views on 115–116
Scottish nationalism, views on 130–131
visual art 10
Gunn, Neil 103

H

Habermas, Jurgen 35
A History Maker (Gray novel) 98–100, 116, 119
Hobbes, Thomas 17
Horkheimer, Max 32–34
Hume, David 26–27
Hume, Kathryn 67

I

inferiorism. *See* Scottish literary criticism

J

Jackson, Rosemary 67, 73
Jameson, Fredric 118–120
Jenkins, Robin 45–46
Julius, Anthony 30

K

Kaczvinsky, Donald P. 15, 133
Kant, Immanuel 103, 107, 118
Kearney, Richard 29, 126
Kennedy, A.L. 46–47
King, Elspeth 10
kinship. *See* communion
Kirsner, Douglas 88–89
Klinkowitz, Jerome 121

L

Lacan, Jacques 119
Laing, R.D. *See* psychoanalysis
Lanark (Gray novel)
   alienation effect 108–112

chronological time 106
dragonhide/depersonalisation 55–56, 64–65, 78, 87
fantastic (Todorov's sense) 84–85
Graves, Robert, intertextual with 30, 36–40
personal relations 41–44, 53, 65
postmodern reading of 21, 87
providentialism 94, 97
Scottish masculinity 23–24, 27
sexual repression 55–56
lunar imagery 24–28
Lawrence, D.H. *See* primitivism
Leonard, Tom 58, 75
Lumsden, Alison 112, 116

M

Macmurray, John 19
Mailer, Norman 122
Mangan, Gerald 11
Marcus, Steven 76
Marx, Karl 17
Massie, Alan 11
McCarthy, Patrick 123
McCrone, David 130–131
McHale, Brian 15, 85
Merrill, Robert 124
Miller, Gavin 14, 20
Mitchison, Naomi 59

N

narration
   Brechtian alienation 108–112
   modernist temporality 100–107
   providentialism 93–100
      world history 96–100
   temporal phenomenalism 102–112
   transcendent perspective 92–93
national religion. *See* communion

P

Poor Things (Gray novel) 80–83
postmodernism
   Gray scholarly criticism 15–16, 87, 115–120
   re-interpreted in Vonnegut, Kurt 120–124
postnationalism 125–132

Pound, Ezra. *See* primitivism
primitivism
  "The Great Bear Cult" (Gray short story) 30
  Auden, W.H. 35
  Eliot, T.S. 29–30
  Frazer, J.G. 28–30
  Graves, Robert
  Lanark, intertextual with 36–44
  poetic theory 30–36
  Lawrence, D.H. 29
  Pound, Ezra 30
  Yeats, W.B. 29–30
Proust, Marcel 101–104
  involuntary memory 102–104
psychoanalysis 53–86
  Fairbairn, W.R.D. 69–71
  Freud, Sigmund 17, 70
  fantasy 67
  Laing, R.D.
    anti-psychiatry 53
    communion 61
    depersonalisation 64–66
    divided/schizoid self 20, 68, 72
    fantasy 77–80
    Gray's literature, application to 57–68, 74–86
    hermeneutic method 61
    interpersonal method 62–66
    metanoia 74–76
    Reich, Wilhelm, contrast with 66
    Sartre, Jean-Paul, relation to 88–91
    Scottish literature, influence on 57–59
    subjectivity 84
  Reich, Wilhelm 55–57
  Suttie, Ian 71

R

reading. *See* communion
recognition. *See* communion
"A Report to the Trustees of the Bellahouston Travelling Scholarship" (Gray memoir) 75
Rycroft, Charles 56

S

sacrifice. *See* communion
Sartre, Jean-Paul 88–95
  Kantian temporality, critique of 107
  Laing, R.D., similarities 88
  reading and temporality 91, 100
  What is Literature? 91
  Words 90–93
Scholl, Peter A. 124
Schopenhauer, Arthur 95, 102–103
Scottish literary criticism
  essentialism 13–14, 125–126
  inferiorism 14
  traditionalism 12–13
Scottish Renaissance 14–15
Scriven, Anne 13
Shepherd, Nan 19, 50–52
Sixteen Occasional Poems: 1990–2000 (Gray poetry) 115
Smith, Anthony D. 127–128
Smith, G. Gregory 13
Smith, Martin Seymour 30
Smith, William Robertson. *See* communion
Something Leather (Gray novella) 12, 59, 68–69, 72
Spark, Muriel 95
"The Start of the Axletree", "The End of the Axletree" (Gray short stories) 129
Stenhouse, David 55
Stevenson, Randall 102, 108
Sutherland, John 11
Suttie, Ian. *See* psychoanalysis

T

temporal phenomenalism. *See* narration
Ten Tales Tall and True (Gray short story collection) 9
Tiitinen, Johanna 116, 117
Todorov, Tzvetan 83
Tolstoy, Leo 97–98

V

van Gennep, Arnold 48. *See* communion
Vickery, John B. 29
Vonnegut, Kurt 120–124

W

White, Hayden 116–118
Whyte, Christopher 13

Why Scots Should Rule Scotland (Gray pamphlet) 88, 96, 130–131
Working Legs (Gray drama) 58

Y

Young, Elizabeth 11